# Lo𝒯us ℐllustrated
# DICTIONARY
## *of*
# ARCHAEOLOGY

*Complied and Edited by:*
**Stephen Armstrong**

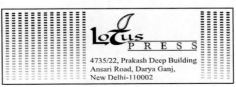

4735/22, Prakash Deep Building
Ansari Road, Darya Ganj,
New Delhi-110002

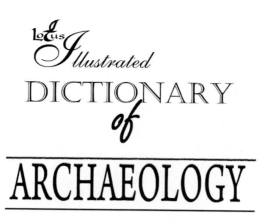

# Lotus Illustrated
# DICTIONARY
## of
# ARCHAEOLOGY

© Lotus Press: 2023

*ISBN 81 89093 11 8*

Published by:
**Lotus Press : Publishers & Distributors**
Unit No. 220, 2nd Floor, 4735/22,
Prakash Deep Building, Ansari Road, Darya Ganj,
New Delhi- 110002, Ph.: 41325510, 09811838000
• E-mail : lotuspress1984@gmail.com www.lotuspress.co.in

*Printed & Published by :* **Lotus Press Publisher & Distributors,** New Delhi-02

# PREFACE

The scientific study of the physical evidence of past human societies recovered through the excavation. Archaeology not only attempts to discover and describe past cultures, but also to formulate explanations for the development of cultures.

Archaeology involves controlled methods of survey and excavation, aimed at recovering objects and remains, which provide information about the structures and activities of people in the past. The relationships of these objects and remains can be reconstructed and aspects of their cultural meaning determined. Since so much of the material, which survives the passage of time consists of tools, weapons and other implements, archaeologists attach great importance to the technologies of vanished peoples.

Archaeologists use various terms to describe their finds. Items which were deliberately fashioned to serve some purpose, such as tools and ornaments, are called 'artifacts' and the whole collection of artifacts from any given site is called an 'assemblage'. Structures, including remains of dwellings and food processing and cooking areas, are called 'features'. The term, 'samples', refers to controlled collections of bones, seeds, shells, soils and wood ash.

This book is a collection of all terms used in archaeology. It also defines the various types of artifacts like chopper, hand axes, microliths etc.

## a.d.
represents years in the Christian era. anno domini.

## aborigine
a native human inhabitant of a country or geographic area. In North America, the native North American Indian.

## abrading stone
a stone, typically sandstone or limestone, used to smooth or sharpen antler, bone, wood and other stone.

## abrasive stone
usually a sandstone slab used for grinding and polishing.

## absolute dating
the determination of age with reference to a specific time scale, such as a fixed calendrical system. Also referred to as chronometric dating.

## abutment
masonry platform or earth embankment, supporting the central structure of a bridge.

## acanthodians
a primitive group of Silurian to Permian jawed bony fishes, bearing bony spines in front of all but their caudal fins.

## accession file
file that contains the documentation for each incoming repository transaction, including all legal records. Often includes the documentation of a de-accession.

## accession number
a unique number assigned to a collection or, in some cases, an object for the purposes of identification not description.

## accession register
system, either in manual/paper form and/or electronic form, used by repositories to keep track of all accessions.

■ **accession/ accessioning**

the formal and legal documentation of an incoming repository transaction, including a gift, purchase, exchange, transfer or field collection. Also includes establishment of legal title and/or custody.

■ **acetone**

a colourless, highly flammable liquid that is soluble in water. Commonly used as a solvent for adhesives.

■ **achieved status**

social standing and prestige, reflecting the ability of an individual to acquire an established position in society, as a result of individual accomplishments.

■ **acid-free**

a material that has a pH of 7.0 or higher (an alkaline), since acids can weaken cellulose in paper, cloth and board and lead to embrittlement.

■ **acquisition/ acquisitioning**

a process to obtain custody of an object, document or collection that involves physical transfer.

■ **acryloid b72**

acrylic resin used as a consolidant, as a barrier material or base coat to label objects and as an adhesive.

■ **active stabilisation**

interventionist treatment action taken to increase the stability or durability of an object.

■ **activity area**

a limited portion of a site in which a specialised cultural function was carried out, such as food preparation, tool manufacture, etc.

■ **acute**

severe short angles coming to a sharp point.

■ **adaptation**

changes in gene frequencies resulting from selective pressures being placed upon a population by environmental factors. It results in a greater fitness of the population to its ecological niche. In other words, adaptation is the acclimatisation to better fit with the environmental conditions or other external stimuli.

■ **adena**

the major cultural group of the woodland period. The adena had cultural influences in Indiana, Kentucky, Maryland, New York, Ohio, Pennsylvania and West Virgina. The adena are regarded in modern times as being accomplished craftsmen.

■ **adze**

a tool, typically made from stone, that was presumed to be used like a modern woodworker's chisel to work wood.

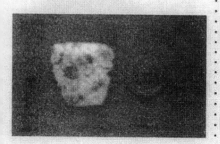

■ **adze-blade**

a ground and polished stone artefacts characterised by a generally rectangular shape with a bevelled cutting edge on one end. Used as a woodworking tool.

0 1 2 3
cm

35C05/#2208

■ **aerial photography**

photographic coverage of the land surface obtained from the air. Useful in locating and recording site positions.

■ **aerial reconnaissance**

an important survey technique in the discovery and recording of archaeological sites.

# aerial thermography

a non-photographic technique which uses thermal or heat sensors in aircraft to record the temperature of the soil surface. Variations in soil temperature can be the result of the presence of buried structures. It uses the differences in the radiation of heat from the ground to determine where burial sites are located.

# agate

a semi-precious chalcedony formed as quartz fossils of a previous geological age. The colours of agate can be clouded, clear or banded.

# agger

inclined embankment-mound carrying a Roman road.

# ala

unit of cavalry in the Roman auxiliary army.

# alamanni

a tribe in Southern Germany, which lived the time between 260 AD and 750 AD.

# albian

European stage of the uppermost Lower Cretaceous, spanning the time between 107 and 95 million years ago.

# algae

photosynthetic, almost exclusively aquatic, nonvascular plants that range in size from simple unicellular form to giant kelps several feet long. They have extremely varied life cycles and first appeared in the Precambrian.

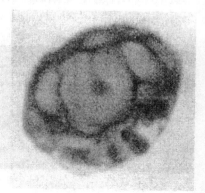

# alidade

an optical surveying instrument used in conjunction with a plane-table and stadia-rod to produce detailed large-scale topographic maps.

# alloying

a technique involving the mixing of two or more metals to create an entirely new material, e.g. the fusion of copper and tin to make bronze.

# alluvial fan

a cone-shaped deposit of sediments generally formed where a mountain stream discharges onto a level surface. Alluvial fan deposits are among the most common surficial sediments in mountainous terrain.

# alluvium

sediments (mud, sand and gravel) laid down by flowing water. The largest particles (sand and gravel) tend to accumulate within the channel itself. Particles of clay, silt and fine sand are small enough to be suspended in flowing water. When the stream overflows its banks, these particles can be distributed across the valley floor. These overbank or flood deposits are the most common contexts in which buried archaeological sites are found. Stream valley floors

are underlain by deposits of alluvium and often contain buried archaeological sites.

# alternate

when used in reference to a flaked projectile or tool, alternate implies that the opposite face of opposing edges was flaked.

# altimeter

a barometric device for determining elevations above sea-level.

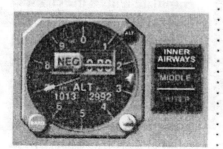

# altithermal

a postulated climatic period characterised by warmer and/or drier conditions approximately 4,000-8,000 years ago.

# ambulatory

covered portico surrounding the inner shrine of a temple.

# amino-acid racemisation

a method used in the dating of both human and animal bone. Its significance is that with a small sample (10g), it can be applied to material up to 100,000 years old, i.e. beyond the time range of radiocarbon dating.

# ammonite

a coiled, chambered fossil shell of a cephalopod mollusc of the extinct order Ammonoidea.

# amoeba

a microscopic, unicellular animal, consisting of a naked mass of protoplasm.

# analogy

a process of reasoning, whereby two entities sharing some similarities are assumed to share many others.

# ancillary sample

any non-artefactual material collected by archaeologists, to aid in dating, palaeo-environmental reconstruction or other interpretations - e.g. carbon samples, soil samples, palynological samples, etc.

# annealing

in copper and bronze metallurgy, this refers to the repeated process of heating and hammering the material to produce the desired shape.

# anthropology

the study of humanity - our physical characteristics as animals and our unique non-biological characteristics that we call culture. The scientific and humanistic study of man's present and past biological, linguistic, social and cultural variations. Its major sub fields are archaeology, physical anthropology, cultural anthropology and anthropological linguistics.

# anthropomorphic

'man-like'. Used to describe artefacts or artwork decorated with human features or with a man-like appearance.

# antiquarian

one who studies the past as a hobby rather than as a profession.

# anvil

a rock that was used as a level base for chipping other stone into tools, blades or projectile points. Typically part of a flint knapper's toolkit.

■ **aperture**

a relatively large opening on the last-formed chamber of a foraminiferal shell.

■ **apodyterium**

undressing room in a bath-suite.

■ **appraisal**

the process of determining the monetary value of an item.

■ **aptian**

European stage of the Lower Cretaceous, spanning the time between 114 and 107 million years ago.

■ **arbitrary level**

an excavation level defined by factors of convenience, with no necessary relationship to site-stratigraphy or cultural components.

■ **archaean**

the middle era of Precambrian time, spanning the period between 3.8 and 2.5 billion years ago. Life arose on Earth during the early Archaean, as indicated by the appearance of fossil bacteria in rocks thought to be about 3.5 billion years old. Its name means 'ancient'.

■ **archaeobotany**

see **paleoethnobotany**.

■ **archaeological context**

the physical setting, location and cultural association of artefacts and features within an archaeological site.

■ **archaeological culture**

a constantly recurring assemblage of artefacts, assumed to be representative of a particular set of behavioural activities carried out at a particular time and place (cf. culture).

■ **archaeologist**

a scientist who studies the remains of past and present

humans trained in the knowledge and methods of archaeology. A professional archaeologist usually holds a degree in anthropology, with a specialisation in archaeology, and is trained to collect archaeological information in a 'proper' scientific way.

## ■ archaeology

the scientific study of the physical evidence of past human societies, recovered through collection, artefact analysis and excavation. Archaeologists not only attempt to discover and describe past cultures but also formulate explanations for the development of cultures. Conclusions drawn from study and analysis provide answers and predictions about human behaviour that add, complement and sometimes correct the written accounts of history and prehistory.

## ■ archaeology of cult

the study of the material indications of patterned actions undertaken in response to religious beliefs.

## ■ archaeomagnetic dating

sometimes referred to as paleo-magnetic dating. It is based on the fact that changes in the earth's magnetic field over time can be recorded as remnant magnetism in materials such as baked clay structure (ovens, kilns and hearths).

## ■ archaeozoology

at times, referred to as zoo-archaeology, this involves the identification and analysis of faunal species from archaeological sites, as an aid to the reconstruction of human diets and to an understanding of the contemporary environment at the time of deposition.

## archaic period

a time frame in North American pre-history spanning 7,000 years between 10,000 b.p. to 3000 b.p., after paleo and before woodland times. The 7,000 years is further defined as early, middle and late archaic.

## archaic

new world time period known for its permanent settlements and the transformation to an agrarian economy from one of hunting and gathering.

## architrave

the horizontal member above two columns (piers, etc.), spanning the interval between them.

## archival quality

materials that have been manufactured of inert materials specifically designed to extend the life of artefact and records by protecting them from agents of deterioration.

## archives

1. the permanently valuable non-current records of an organisation, with their original order and provenance intact, maintained by the original organisation.
2. the organisation that created and holds the records.
3. the physical building/room in which the records are held.

## archivist

person professionally educated, trained and engaged in

the administration and management of archival and manuscript collections.

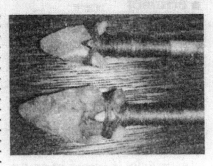

## ■ arrowhead or arrowpoint

a weapon point or tip made of stone, bone, metal or other material, which, in general, is less than 2 1/2 inches in length (63 mm) and attributed no earlier than the woodland phase of north American aborigine prehistory. Larger points are regarded as spear points or knife blades and are associated with spear and dart, atlatl or hand thrown delivery systems for hafted cutting.

## ■ art object

any artefact carrying or consisting of, decorative or artistic elements.

## ■ articulated

two or more bones left in their anatomical position after tissue decay.

# ■ artefact

an old, authentic object used, crafted or manufactured by the application of human workmanship or activity, especially one of prehistoric origin that may have archaeological significance especially if found in an undisturbed context. A manually portable product of human workmanship. In its broadest sense, it includes tools, weapons, ceremonial items, art objects, all industrial waste and all floral and faunal remains modified by human activity. Common examples include projectile points, tools, utensils, art, food remains and other products of human activity.

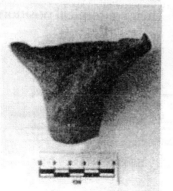

# ■ ascribed status

social standing or prestige which is the result of inheritance or hereditary factors.

# ■ assemblage

a group of artefacts which represent a culture. A group of artefacts related to each other based upon some recovery from a common archaeological context. Also a group of artefacts recurring together at a particular time and place and representing the sum of human activities. Assemblage examples are artefacts from a site or feature.

# ■ assessment, collections

the process of evaluating a collection for the purpose of documenting its condition, relating it to the mission and goals of the repository and determining courses of action regarding its care and management.

# ■ associated records

original records (or copies thereof) that are prepared, assembled and that document the efforts to locate, evaluate, record, study, preserve or recover a prehistoric or historic resource.

# ■ association

the co-occurrence of an artefact with other archaeological remains, usually in the same matrix.

# ■ asymmetrical

when used in reference to projectiles or tools, asymmetrical refers to the opposing side of an object which has dissimilar contours, shape or form.

# ■ atlatl

1. the aztec word for a spear throwing stick device. This projectile propulsion device preceded the bow and arrow. In general, a wooden or bone stick or board with a handgrip at one end and a spur or hook at the other end. The atlatl is used as an extension of the arm in throwing a spear or dart. The spear shaft is socketed and fits into the spur or hook of the atlatl. Essentially, the atlatl lengthens the length of the spear thrower's arm and with loaded, spring-like motion can provide the benefit of greater force and distance over that of the hand thrown spear. It is hypothesised that sometimes a stone weight(s) (a.k.a.: bannerstone, birdstone, boatstone) was attached to the atlatl to provide better balance or to load the device with a spring or bending effect or to diminish the

'whoosh' noise created during the throwing process.

2. a bone or wood shaft implement, held in one hand and used to propel a spear. The tool functions as a lever, giving greater thrust and distance to the spear or dart being thrown.

■ **atlatl-weight**

usually, a ground and polished stone object with grooves or perforations - for attachment to the shaft of an atlatl. Presumed to play role in the balancing of the weapon while throwing.

■ **Atomic Absorption Spectrometry (AAS)**

a method of analysing artefact composition similar to optical emission spectrometry (OES), in that it measures energy in the form of visible light waves. It is capable of measuring up to 40 different elements with an accuracy of c. 1 percent.

■ **attribute**

a minimal characteristic of an artefact such that it cannot be further subdivided. The attributes commonly studied include aspects of form, style, decoration, colour and raw material.

■ **attritional age profile**

a mortality pattern based on bone or tooth wear which is characterised by an overrepresentation of young and old animals in relation to their numbers in live populations. It suggests either scavenging of attritional mortality victims (i.e. those dying from natural causes or from non-human predation) or the hunting by humans or other predators of the most vulnerable individuals.

■ **augering**

a subsurface detection method using either a hand or machine-powered drill to determine the depth and character of archaeological deposits.

## ■ auricle

the corners of a stem of stemmed types or the corners of the base of triangular types which are ear-like.

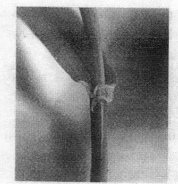

## ■ auriculate

a major projectile form which has rounded or pointed ears that project from the concave base or stem of points or blades.

## ■ authentic

true or genuine. Artefacts made in prehistoric times.

## ■ awl

a small pointed hand tool used for piercing holes in leather, wood and other materials

## ■ axe

a large chopping tool that may have a grove for hafting to a handle.

## ■ azimuth

a magnetic bearing sighted from your position to a known landmark. Used in navigation and in determining site locations.

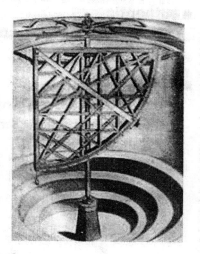

■ **b.c.**

a year some time before the birth of Christ. The pre Christian era.

■ **b.p.**

1. before present. Where present is defined as the year 1950 a.d. therefore, 1949 b.p. would be the year 1 a.d. and 1951 b.p. would be the year 2. the notation commonly used on radiocarbon dates, e.g. 1,000 B.P. = 1,000 years before 1950 A.D. or approximately 1,000 A.D.

■ **back dirt**

the excavated material from a site, presumed to be of little or no further archaeological significance.

■ **back-filling**

the process of refilling a completed excavation.

■ **backing**

material used to support fragile objects, usually attached by adhesives. Backing may be made of either flexible or rigid materials, but should always be able to expand and contract in a similar manner as the object it supports. It should also be reversible.

■ **bailey**

fortified enclosure in a medieval castle.

■ **ballista**

artillery- weapon discharging arrows and stone balls.

# band

a small territorially based social group consisting of 2 or more nuclear families. A loosely integrated population, sharing a sense of common identity but few specialised institutions.

# banner stone

1. a stone that was attached to an atl atl in order to make it a more effective weapon by adding weight and balance.

2. a stone presumed to be an atlatl weight with a drilled centred hole or a grove. The bannerstone could be a ceremonial object and remains a problematical artefact. Certain bannerstones are so large and elaborate that their design and size totally precludes them from being used effectively as an atlatl weight and thus are considered ceremonial objects.

# barb

1. a sharp backwards extension of a projectile point intended to act as a hook to keep the point within a wound.

2. a sharp protrusion of the blade of stemmed or notched types at the proximal corners. There are 6 major types of barbs, *expanded* which means flaring outward and upwards towards the distal end, *horizontal* which means flaring outward at 90 degrees to the stem, *inversely tapered* which means pointing downward and getting thinner, *rounded* which means the outline is semi-circular, *struck* which means knocked off and *tapered* which means minimised in an angle towards the tip.

# barremian

European stage of the Lower Cretaceous, spanning the time between 118 and 114 million years ago.

■ **barrow**

a large mound of earth or stones placed over a burial. The term is especially used in reference to the mounds of England.

■ **basal edge**

the proximal edge of a triangular or lanceolate projectile or stem of a stemmed type. There are eight major types of basal edges: *convex, straight, concave, auriculate, lobbed, bifurcated, fractured* and *snapped.*

■ **basal grinding**

intentional smoothing of the base or stem of a chipped stone projectile point.

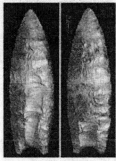

■ **basal thinning**

the intentional removal of small, longitudinal flakes from the basal edge of a pro-jectile point, in order that the tool or point could be more easily hafted or held.

■ **basalt**

a fine-grained volcanic rock used for the manufacture of chipped stone artefacts. Colour: black to grey. Texture: granular to glass-like.

■ **base**

the base is the proximal or end portion of a knife, tool or projectile point. The base is usually designed for hafting or gripping, but not designed or intended for cutting, scraping or penetrating. Often at times, base edges were ground so that sharp edges would not abrade the hafting materials and cause hafting failure with use. The bottom part of a knife.

### ■ base-line

an arbitrary line established by stakes and string or by surveying instrument, from which measurements are taken to produce a site-map or to provide an initial axis for an excavation grid.

### ■ basilica

town hall.

### ■ baulks

unexcavated 'walls' which may be left between pits to provide stratigraphic control.

### ■ bearing

in mapping or navigation, a compass direction or horizontal angle of sight measured in magnetic degrees.

■ **behaviour**

the way a person acts.

■ **bench mark (b.m.)**

a vertical datum-point usually at a known elevation above sea-level, to which mapped elevations may be related.

■ **benthic**

used to describe aquatic organisms that are bottom dwelling.

■ **bentonites**

a clay formed by the decomposition of volcanic ash, having the ability to absorb large quantities of water and to expand to several times its normal volume.

■ **bequest**

transfer of property to an institution under the terms of a deceased person's will.

■ **berm**

in military defences, the level space between two features (e.g. ditch and rampart).

■ **berriasian**

European stage of the lowermost Lower Cretaceous, spanning the time between 135 and 131 million years ago.

■ **bevel, biface**

a bevel which was formed by removing flakes from both faces of an edge.

■ **bevel, steep**

a bevel of a blade edge or stem edge which was flaked at a steep (> 40 degree) angle to the plane of the face.

■ **bevel, uniface**

a bevel which was formed by removing seep flakes from just one face of an edge. The opposing face may have a few flat flake scars of the primary flaking of scattered retouch flake scars.

■ **bevelled**

bevelled refers to a blade edge, a stem side edge or a stem base which was steeply flaked across one or more faces and that produces a noticeable slope.

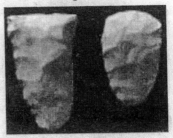

■ **biconical drilling**

a means of perforating beads or pendants for suspension. Accomplished by drilling in from both sides with a tapered drill, resulting in an hour-glass-shaped hole.

■ **biconvex**

a blade shape having two worked faces.

■ **biface**

in reference to projectiles or tools, biface describes those examples which have been worked and exhibit flake scars along both faces or sides.

■ **bifacial flaking**
the manufacture of a stone artefact by removing flakes from both faces.

■ **bifurcated base**
a type of basal stem of a projectile or tool which has a central notch splitting the stem into the form of two ears.

■ **bilaterally barbed**
a projectile point or harpoon with barbs on both edges.

■ **bilaterally symmetrical**
the condition in which, when something is cut down the middle, the two halves formed are generally mirror images of each other.

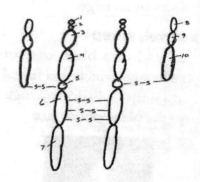

■ **billet**
a bone or antler tool used for flaking.

■ **biological anthropology**
see **physical anthropology**.

■ **bioluminescence**
the production of light by living organisms.

# biostratigraphy

the branch of geology concerned with the separation and differentiation of rock units by means of the study of the fossils they contain.

# bipoint

a bone or stone artefact pointed at both ends.

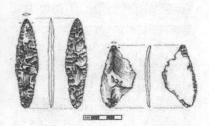

# bipolar percussion

a means of manufacturing chipped stone artefacts, accomplished by placing the raw material on a large rock and hitting it with a hammer stone from above.

# birdstone

typically, a stone artefact, thought to be an atlatl weight which was shaped like a bird. Quite possibly it is some other type of ceremonial object. Some birdstones have bulging or 'pop' eyes, usually made from a banded slate.

# bison jump

a specialised animal trap used on the plains, involving driving bison (or buffalo) over a natural cliff or embankment.

# bivalve

a mollusc having two shells hinged together, as the oyster, clam or mussel or any animal with two halves to its shell, such as an ostracode or brachiopod.

# ■ blade

**1.** overall, this term is used to describe a knife form. However, in lithic projectile terms, the blade is the distal (above the hafting or gripping area) portion of a projectile, knife, axe or other similar tool. Blade is also used to refer to large bifaced flaked artefacts.

**2.** a long slender prismatic flake manufactured by indirect percussion or pressure from a prepared core. It is at least twice as long as it is wide.

# ■ blank

an 'advanced' preliminary stage in the manufacture of an artefact.

# ■ blowout

a patch of land in the great plains states of north America where dry soil is blown away by wind leaving heavier rock and possibly artefacts on the surface.

# ■ blunt

a point that abruptly terminates part way up the blade with no true distal point for piercing. Typically, the point is chipped in a mild excurvate or straight edge. Some feel that the point may have been used in hunting as a 'stunning' weapon, however most blunts show signs as being a conserved, former projectile, reworked into a hand held or hafted scraper.

# ■ boatstone

a stone artefact, shaped like a watercraft, which is thought to be a type of atlatl weight or a ceremonial ornament of some type.

■ **body sherd**
any fragment of a ceramic vessel not identifiable as a rim sherd.

■ **bonding-course**
bands of brickwork (or occasionally stone slabs) which alternate with wider sections of regular stonework. They normally run through the entire thickness of the wall, presumably to give cohesion and stability to the mortared rubble-core. They were also useful as levelling courses during construction.

■ **bone breccia**
cave fill that consists of masses of bone cemented together with calcium carbonate that has dissolved out of limestone.

■ **bone hammer**
a bone that is used as a hammer in the removal of flakes from a core, in the manufacturing of stone tools.

■ **bone industry**
all the bone artefacts from a particular site.

■ **bony fishes**
fish of the class Osteichthyes, characterised by a skeleton composed of bone, in addition to cartilage, gill covers and an air bladder.

■ **boreal forest**
'sub-arctic forest'. A dense mixed forest dominated by spruce, aspen and birch with areas of muskeg. It extends as far north as the tree line i.e. edge of the tundra and is the largest single vegetation zone in Canada.

■ **bosing or bowsing**
a subsurface detection method performed by striking the ground with a heavy wooden mallet or a lead-filled container on a long handle.

■ **botanist**
A person who pursues the scientific study of the structure, growth and identification of plants.

■ **boulder arrangement**
(also boulder mosaic, petroform) surface boulders aboriginally arranged into geometric, zoomorphic or anthropomorphic patterns.

■ **brain endocasts**
these are made by pouring latex rubber into a skull, so as to produce an accurate image of the inner surface of the cranium. This method gives an estimate of cranial capacity and has been used on early hominid skulls.

■ **breaking chain**
the process of obtaining horizontal distances over sloping terrain with a surveyor's chain by measuring stepped level intervals up the slope.

■ **break-in-slope**
any abrupt change in the gradient of a topographic surface, such as the edge of a cliff, terrace scarp, etc.

■ **breastwork**
the vertical timber-work built on top of the earth rampart of a fort to provide screening for the sentry.

■ **brochure**
promotional literature.

■ **brunton compass**
a sophisticated magnetic compass used as a basic surveying instrument. Also known as the 'Brunton Pocket Transit'.

■ **buffer**
a substance containing both a weak acid and its conjugal base, used to restrain the acid migration of a material. Acid-free paper products are often buffered.

■ **bulb of percussion**

1. a bulb resulting from a conchoidal fracture of stone.
2. a raised rounded area on the ventral surface of a conchoidal flake, directly below the striking platform.

■ **bulbar depression**

a depression left from the bulb of percussion when a blade or flake is struck from a core.

■ **bulbous**

a term used to define a stem form that has oval sides and a flat to slightly rounded basal edge.

■ **bundle burial**

human bones bundled together in some material and buried.

■ **burial mound**

mound under which a person or group of people were buried.

■ **burial mound**

an artificial aboriginal mound containing or covering human burials.

■ **burial**

a human interment. May be 'flexed' or 'extended', single or multiple, primary or secondary.

■ **burin**

a tool flaked into a chisel point for inscribing or grooving bone, wood, leather, stone or antler.

■ **burin**

a type of chipped stone artefact, characterised by the deliberate removal of small prismatic flakes i.e. burin spalls down one or more edges. Commonly assumed to have served as engraving or carving tools.

■ **butchering station**

a site or localised activity area within a site, dominated by evidence for the past butchering of game animals, e.g. broken and cut faunal remains and butchering tools.

■ **cache**

a deliberate store of equipment, food, furs or other

resources, placed in, or on the ground perhaps protected by a rock cairn or raised above the ground on a platform deposited in the same safe place, usually of the same type or lithic origin.

■ **cadastre (cadaster)**

a public record of the extent, value and ownership of land within a district for purposes of taxation.

■ **caddo**

a shortened form of the tribal name cadohadacho, referring to three main native American tribal groups spread along wide fertile prairies bordering the great bend in the red river. The three cultures are- the cadohadacho and the natchitoches along the red river and the hasinai along the banks of the upper Neches and Angelina rivers in east Texas. Each tribe within these three regional groupings had

an individual identity and was independently governed, but all had a common language followed the same social and religious customs and shared traditions. Their direct descendants are listed on the tribal roll of the caddo indian tribe of Oklahoma, in the twentieth century.

■ **caddoan culture area**

the geographical region that encompasses eastern Oklahoma, Southwestern Arkansas, western Louisiana and eastern Texas which was the homeland of the native American caddo people.

■ **caddoan**

a family of north American Indian languages, spoken in

the upper Missouri valley in north Dakota, in the Platto valley in Nebraska, in South-western Arkansas and in neighbouring parts of Oklahoma, Texas and Louisiana.

■ **caecilians**
wormlike, almost blind, tropical amphibians of the order Apoda.

■ **cairn**
stones intentionally piled by humans.

■ **calcareous concretions**
a rounded mass of mineral matter occurring in sandstone, clay, etc., often in concentric layers around a nucleus.

■ **calcareous nannofossils**
fossil remains of calcareous nannoplankton.

■ **calcareous nanno-plankton**
protists that normally produce coccoliths during some phase in their life cycle.

■ **calcareous**
of, containing or like calcite (calcium carbonate).

■ **calcined bone**
burned bone reduced to white or blue mineral constituents.

■ **calcite**
a common rock-forming mineral: $CaCO_3$. Calcite can be white, colourless or pale shades of grey, yellow and blue. It readily effervesces (bubbles) in hydrochloric acid and is the principal component of limestone.

■ **caldarium**

hot room (moist heat) in a bath-suite.

■ **calendrical system**

a system of measuring time that is based on natural recurring units of time, such as revolutions of the earth around the sun. The number of such units, which have preceded or elapsed with reference to a specific point in time, determines time.

■ **callche**

a white or tan calcium deposit that can form on artefacts which are found in Texas and adjoining states.

■ **cambrian**

the earliest period of the Paleozoic era, spanning the time between 544 and 505 million years ago. It is named after Cambria, the Roman name for Wales, where rocks of this age were first studied.

■ **campanian**

European stage of the Upper Cretaceous, spanning the time between 84 and 72 million years ago.

■ **carbon sample**

a quantity of organic material, usually charcoal, collected for radiocarbon dating.

■ **carboniferous**

a period of time in the Palaeozoic era that includes the Pennsylvanian and Mississippian periods and extended from 360 to 286 million years ago.

■ **cardinal directions**

north, south, east, west.

■ **cartilaginous fishes**

fish having a skeleton composed mostly of cartilage, as sharks and rays. Cartilage is gristle or a firm, elastic, flexible type of connective tissue.

■ **catalogue**

a systematic listing of objects or groups of associated records with descriptive details, including provenience information.

# catalogue number

a number assigned to all items recovered by archaeological research, to cross-index them to the catalogue.

# catastrophe theory

a branch of mathematical topology developed by Rene Thom, which is concerned with the way in which nonlinear interactions within systems can produce sudden and dramatic effects. Ills argued that there are only a limited number of ways in which such changes can take place and these are defined as elementary catastrophes.

# catastrophic age profile

a mortality pattern based on bone or tooth wear analysis and corresponding to a 'natural' age distribution in which the older the age group, the fewer the individuals it has. This pattern is often found in contexts such as flash floods, epidemics or volcanic eruptions.

# cation-ratio dating

this method aspires to the direct dating of rock carvings and engravings and is also potentially applicable to Palaeolithic artefacts, with a strong patina caused by exposure to desert dust. It depends on the principle that cations of certain elements are more soluble than others, they leach out of rock varnish more rapidly than the less soluble elements and their concentration decreases with time.

# catlinite

another name for pipestone, a reddish sandstone used by Native Americans for making pipes.

# cella

inner shrine of a temple.

■ **cellulose nitrate film**

a flexible film base used for motion picture film and photographic negatives, between about 1890 and 1955. This film base self-destructs over time going through five stages of deterioration. The film should be handled with gloves, foldered in buffered sleeves, boxed, placed in ziplock bags and moved to off-site (non-museum storage) cold storage in a freezer.

■ **celt**

a small axe-like type of stone implement with a sharp edge used for cutting or chopping, probably hafted into a wooden handle, usually held in the hand.

■ **cemetary**

a location where individuals are buried.

■ **cenomanian**

European stage of the lowermost Upper Cretaceous, spanning the time between 95 and 91 million years ago.

■ **cenote**

a ritual well, for example, at the late Maya site of Chichen Itza, into which enormous quantities of symbolically rich goods had been deposited.

■ **cenozoic**

an era of geologic time, from the beginning of the Tertiary period (65 million years ago) to the present. Its name is from Greek and means 'new life'.

■ **central hall**

a frame house consisting of two rooms and an enclosed central hall. When this house type is two storied, it is called an 'I' house.

■ **central place theory**

developed by the geographer Christaller to explain the spacing and function of the settlement landscape. Under idealised conditions, he argued, central places of the same size and nature would be equidistant from each other, surrounded by secondary centres with their own smaller satellites. In spite of its limitations, central place theory has found useful applications in archaeology as a preliminary heuristic device.

■ **centuria**
unit of 80 legionary soldiers, commanded by a centurion.

■ **ceramic**
of or pertaining to pottery.

■ **ceremony**
a gathering of people for a program, usually serious in nature, for a specific purpose.

■ **chain**
a surveying chain or long steel tape-measure, calibrated in metres or feet, used for site mapping and grid layout.

■ **chaine operatoire**
ordered chain of actions, gestures and processes in a production sequence (e.g. of a stone tool or a pot) which led to the transformation of a given material towards the finished product. The concept, introduced by Andre Leroi-Gourhan, is significant in allowing the archaeologist to infer back from the finished artefact to the procedures, the intentions in the production sequence and ultimately to the conceptual template of the maker.

■ **chalcedony**
a semi-translucent silicate (quartz) rock with a wax-like lustre and a great range of colours, the sources of which are usually nodular. Used as raw material for the manufacture of chipped stone artefacts. Commonly called agate.

■ **channel flake**
a long longitudinal percussion flake removed in the fluting process.

■ **characterisation**

the application of techniques of examination by which characteristic properties of the constituent material of traded goods can be identified and thus their source of origin, e.g. petrographic thin-section analysis.

■ **chert**

1. a fine grained sedimentary rock that is white, pinkish, brown, grey or blue-grey in colour. It is often shaped into stone artefacts by chipping.

2. a mainly opaque, fairly granular, silicate very fine grained rock formed in ancient ocean sediments. It often has a semi-glossy finish and is usually white, pinkish, brown, grey or blue-grey in colour. It can be shaped into arrowheads and projectile by chipping, has often been called flint, but true flint is found in chalk deposits and is a distinctive blackish colour. In north America, high grade glossy cherts are called 'flint', while low grade, dull chert is called 'chert'.

■ **chi- rho**

Christian symbol composed of the first two letters of the Greek name for Christ (Xp-Cros).

■ **chiefdom**

a term used to describe a society that operates on the principle of ranking, i.e. differential social status. Different lineages are graded on a scale of prestige, calculated by how closely related one is to the chief. The chiefdom generally has a permanent ritual and ceremonial centre, as well as being characterised by local specialisation in crafts.

■ **chinampas**

the areas of fertile reclaimed land, constructed by the Aztecs and made of mud dredged from canals.

■ **chi-tho**
crude bifacially flaked boulder spall or slab scraper-cutting tools, commonly associated with northern Athabaskan assemblages, similar to a cortical spall tool.

■ **chopper**
a natural pebble with a crude, steep cutting edge formed by unifacial percussion flaking.

■ **chronology**
the arrangement of events or the materials which represent them, in the order of their occurrence in time.

■ **chronometric dating**
a dating system that refers to a specific point or range of time. Chronometric dates are not necessarily exact dates and they are often expressed as a range.

■ **chronometry**
the art of measuring time accurately.

■ **civitas**
tribal unit.

■ **classic example**
a subjective term used to refer to a specific point specimen which represents the truest form of a particular point type or blade.

■ **classic**
new world time period known for the appearance of urban states in South America.

■ **classification**
the ordering of phenomena into groups or other classificatory schemes on the basis of shared attributes.

■ **clavicula**
in a Roman camp, curved extension of rampart (and ditch) protecting a gateway.

■ **clay**
material used for making pots.

# ■ climap

a project aimed at producing palaeo-climatic maps, showing sea-surface temperatures in different parts of the globe, at various periods.

# ■ clipped wing

a barbed shoulder that has been fractured off or clipped.

# ■ clovis point

large stone projectile point used by early American hunters to kill large game animals.

# ■ cluster

a group of stylistically and chronologically similar artefacts, for which adequate excavation data does not exist, to allow for the classification as a phase.

# ■ cluster analysis

a multivariate statistical technique which assesses the similarities between units or assemblages, based on the occurrence or non-occurrence of specific artefact types or other components within them.

# ■ coccoliths

microscopic structures of varying shape and size that are made of calcite, are secreted by calcareous nannoplankton and are found in marine deposits from the Triassic period to the Recent. Coccoliths range in size from one to thirty-five micrometres in size.

# ■ cognitive map

an interpretive framework of the world which, it is argued, exists in the human mind and affects actions and decisions as well as knowledge structures.

# ■ cognitive-processual approach

an alternative to the materialist orientation of the functional-processual approach, it is concerned with (1) the integration of the cognitive and symbolic with other aspects of early societies (2) the role of ideology as an active organisational force. It employs the theoretical approach of methodological individualism.

# ■ cohort

unit of infantry soldiers, legionary or auxiliary.

# ■ collagen

the organic fraction of bone as distinct from the mineral or carbonate portion. Can be dated by the C-14 method.

# ■ collateral

a term which refers to a flaking style where parallel flakes are removed from each side of the face of a blade and meet in the centre of the blade, forming a median ridge.

# ■ collateral flaking

when flakes on a chipped stone artefact extend to the middle from both edges, forming a medial ridge. The flakes are at right angles to the longitudinal axis, and regular and uniform in size.

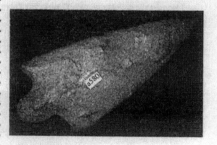

# ■ collecting plan

term used by repositories, it is a document, usually part of a repository's acquisition policy, that specifically details what the repository is going to collect in order to fulfil its mission, goals and scope of collections.

■ **collecting strategy**

a plan that details what is going to be collected during archaeological fieldwork. Can include details on artefact class/type, number, location and sampling.

■ **collection**

material remains that are excavated or removed during a survey, excavation or other study of a prehistoric or historic resource and associated records that are prepared or assembled in connection with the survey, excavation or other study.

■ **collections and data management**

archaeologists work with conservators, curators and computer programmers to catalogue, preserve and store the vast numbers of archaeological artefacts, reports and site records. Storage space for artefacts and records is a continuing problem for many archaeologists and agencies.

■ **collections management**

the management and care of collections with concern for their long term physical well being and safety. Includes issues of conservation, access and use and inventory, as well as management of the overall composition of the collection(s) in relation to the repository's mission and goals.

■ **collections manager**

a trained professional who is responsible for any and all aspects of collections care. Specific responsibilities vary by institution, but can include day-to-day care of and access to collections, cataloguing and information management.

■ **colluvium**

material deposited by gravity at the foot of a slope, e.g. talus, soil creep, etc.

■ **colonia**

settlement of retired legionaries. For York, it is a title of honour.

## compass rose

used to show direction on a map.

## complex

a consistently recurring assemblage of artefacts or traits which may be indicative of a specific set of activities or a common cultural tradition.

## component

the manifestation of a given archaeological phase at a site. Sites may be 'single component' (only one distinct cultural unit) or 'multi-component' (2 or more cultural units).

## composite tool

a tool formed of two or more joined parts, e.g. 'composite toggling harpoon head'.

## compound mound

mounds that are made up of conical mounds connected by linear mounds.

## Computed Axial Tomography (CAT or CT scanner)

the method by which scanners allow detailed internal views of bodies such as mummies. The body is passed into the machine and images of crosssectional 'slices' through the body are produced.

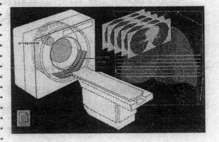

## concave

a term to describe an outline which curves inward. Synonymous with incurvate and the opposite of convex and excurvate, it is suggested that this term only be used to describe basal edges.

## concentration

a notable accumulation of archaeological materials in a small area, such as a 'concentration of flakes', etc.

## conchoidal flake

a type of spall resulting from the fracture of fine-grained or glassy rocks. Characterised by a bulb of percussion, striking platform remnant and extremely sharp edges. A predictable fracture pattern that allows the manufacture of pre-determined tools from these materials.

## conchoidal fracture

a breakage of rock in concentric circles or in a clam shell-like scar pattern, referring to the characteristic fractures resulting from pressure and percussion flaking of flint and chert.

## concretion

a natural clay nodule formed out of solution in soil interstices. Often confused for man-made objects because of their peculiar shapes.

## condition report

an accurate, descriptive report of an object's or document's state of preservation at a moment in time, assists in the planning of conservation treatment.

## conglomerate

a rock composed of rounded pebbles and sand which are cemented together into a solid rock.

## coniacian

European stage of the Upper Cretaceous, spanning the time between 90 and 88 million years ago.

## conical mound

a cone or oval shaped mound that usually contains human burials.

## conjoining

see **refitting**.

## conjunctive approach

a methodological alternative to traditional normative archaeology, argued by Walter Taylor (1948), in which the full range of a cultural system was to be taken into consideration in explanatory models.

# conchoidal theory of flint fracture

the theory that ideally a cone will be punched out of a piece of flint, when it is struck with sufficient force.

# conservation archaeology

a sub-field of archaeology which focuses on the preservation of archaeological resources. This position encourages the stabilisation and preservation of archaeological sites, as opposed to their immediate excavation.

# conservation

measures taken to prolong the life of an object or document and its physical, historic and scientific integrity as long as possible in its original form. May involve chemical stabilisation or physical strengthening. Treatments should be fully tested, reviewed and recorded by professional conservators.

# conservator

a person trained in the theoretical and practical aspects of preventive conservation and in performing treatments to prolong the lives of objects and documents. Often specialises in a particular class of objects or materials.

# consolidant

a chemical used to strengthen the structural material of an object.

# constructed feature

something that is built to provide a setting for activities, e.g. homes, businesses and temples.

# context

the relation of an artefact or cultural remains to the surrounding artefacts or remains and to the soil level in which they were found. The surrounding conditions of an archaeological find. An artefact's context usually consists of its immediate matrix (the material surrounding it, e.g. gravel, clay or sand), its provenience (horizontal and vertical position within the matrix) and its association with other artefacts (occurrence together with other archaeological remains, usually in the same matrix). 'Primary context' refers to materials found in their original position, 'secondary context' refers to material displaced and re-deposited by disturbance factors, 'geological context' is the relationship of the archaeological finds to geological strata.

■ **contextual seriation**
a method of relative dating pioneered by Flinders Petrie in the 19th century, in which artefacts are arranged according to the frequencies of their co-occurrence in specific contexts (usually burials).

■ **contour interval**
the vertical spacing of contour lines on a topographic map - e.g. 10 m , 100 ft., etc..

■ **contour line**
a line on a map connecting points of equal elevation.

■ **contoured level**
an excavation level with a floor parallel to the slope of the ground surface.

■ **contract archaeology**
archaeological research conducted under the aegis of federal or state legislation, often in advance of highway construction or urban development, where the archaeologist is contracted to undertake the necessary research.

■ **contracting**
a term that refers to the width of a stem or point that is diminishing in outline.

■ **control**
in the scientific method, a situation in which a compari-

son can be made between a specific situation and a second situation that differs, ideally, in only one aspect from the first.

■ **convex**

a term to describe an outline which curves outward, synonymous with excurvate and the opposite of concave. It is suggested that this term only be used to describe basal edges.

■ **copper breast ornament**

a piece of pounded natural copper.

■ **coprolites**

fossilised faeces. These contain food residues that can be used to reconstruct diet and subsistence activities.

■ **copyright**

legal recognition of special intellectual property rights, distinct from the right of possession, that a creator may have for their work. Copyright exists for original works in tangible media and covers the rights to reproduce, adapt, distribute, perform or display the work.

■ **core**

1. a 'parent' stone, such as flint or chert, from which flakes or blades have been struck and removed (by percussion) for use in the manufacture of tools or projectiles.

2. a blocky nucleus of stone from which flakes or blades have been removed.

3. a column or lineal sample of materials obtained by 'coring' the ground, trees, etc. Individual cores are brought to the surface for geologic examination and/ or laboratory analysis.

■ **coring**

a type of drilling in which a column of earth is removed and can be studied.

■ **corner notch**

a major projectile form which is described as a point that has had notches for hafting, struck into the corners of the base. Also, a flaking technique applied to accommodate hafting which involved the flaking of notches into the basal corners of a preform base.

■ **corrosion**

an electrochemical process involving gradual destruction of an object, usually metals, through change in the object's material(s).

■ **cortex**

the naturally weathered outer surface of a pebble.

■ **cortical spall**

a flake struck from the surface of a pebble or nodule which retains the natural cortex on one face. A 'Cortical Spall Tool' is generally a relatively large ovate cortical spall exhibiting retouch or use-wear on one or more edges.

■ **cotype**

an example of the original series when there is no holotype, the describer having used a number of examples of equal value.

■ **coulees**

steep sided valleys found along the Upper Mississippi Waterway.

■ **courier**

an individual, usually a representative of an object or document owner or a repository, who travels with an item to ensure its proper care and safe arrival at a venue.

## crazing

a fine mesh of minute cracks on an object's surface. Crazing is most often seen on ceramic glazes and some types of glass.

## creation-science

the idea that scientific evidence can be and has been gathered for creation as depicted in the Bible. Mainstream scientists and the Supreme Court discount any scientific value of creation-science statements.

## cremation

burials that are made from the remains of burned human bones.

## cremation ashes

fragments of charred human bones.

## crescent

a mysterious 1/4 moon shaped artefact found in the great basin area of the United States that may have ben a blade form or a scraper or a transverse hafted projectile point. It is found in one of three types: a crescent moon, a crescent half moon, a crescent butterfly shape.

## cretaceous

the final period of the Mesozoic era, spanning the time between 145 and 65 million years ago. The name is derived from the Latin word for chalk ('creta') and was first applied to extensive deposits of this age that form white cliffs along the English Channel between Great Britain and France.

## critical theory

a theoretical approach developed by the so-called 'Frankfurt School' of German social thinkers, which stresses that all knowledge is historical and in a sense biased communication, thus, all claims to 'objective' knowledge are illusory.

## ■ crizzling

small scale, minute cracking of a material (similar to crazing). In glass, it results from the leaching out of alkalis.

## ■ crop-mark

colour-differentiation in standing crops or vegetation (best seen from the air), indicating the presence of buried ancient features.

## ■ cross section

in reference to a blade, the shape of the blade form if the blade were cut across the blade and perpendicular to the length of the blade.

## ■ cross-hall

covered assembly- area in the headquarters building of a fort.

## ■ cryptocrystalline

a term for glassy rocks which break with a conchoidal fracture, such as obsidian.

## ■ cuestas

a long, low ridge with a relatively steep face, escarpment on one side and a long, gentle slope on the other.

## ■ cuestas

a long, low ridge with a relatively steep face, escarpment on one side and a long, gentle slope on the other.

## ■ culling

the process of selecting and removing objects from a group. Usually, entails the rejection of items with no scientific or historical value to the group.

■ **cultural affiliation**

as defined under NAGPRA, cultural affiliation is 'a relationship of shared group identity which can be reasonably traced historically or prehistorically between a present day Indian tribe or Native Hawaiian organisation and an identifiable earlier group'.

■ **cultural anthropology**

a sub-discipline of anthropology concerned with the non-biological, behavioural aspects of society, i.e. the social, linguistic and technological components underlying human behaviour. Two important branches of cultural anthropology are ethnography (the study of living cultures) and ethnology (which attempts to compare cultures using ethnographic evidence). In Europe, it is referred to as social anthropology.

■ **cultural complex**

a group of traits whose associations in time and space indicate that they were the products of the activities of a specific human group.

■ **cultural deposit**

sediments and materials laid down by or heavily modified by, human activity.

■ **cultural determinism**

the idea that except for reflexes all behaviour is the result of learning.

■ **cultural diffusion**

the spreading of cultural traits, e.g., material object, idea or behaviour pattern from one society to another, through trade or other forms of contact.

■ **cultural drift**

cultural change that is due to the improper passing on of information from the people in one region to those of another. Results in the eventual creation of a new culture.

■ **cultural group**

a complex of regularly occurring associated artefacts, features, burial types and house forms comprising a distinct identity.

■ **cultural materialism**
the theory, espoused by Marvin Harris, that ideas, values and religious beliefs are the means or products of adaptation to environmental conditions ('material constraints').

■ **cultural patrimony (objects of)**
as defined under NAGPRA, an object having ongoing historical, traditional or cultural importance central to the American Indian group or culture itself, rather than property owned by an individual Native American and which, therefore, cannot be alienated, appropriated or conveyed by any individual regardless of whether or not the individual is a member of the Indian tribe or Native Hawaiian organisation and such object shall have been considered inalienable by such Native American group at the time the object was separated from such group.

■ **cultural relativism**
the ability to view the beliefs and customs of other people, within the context of their culture rather than one's own.

■ **cultural resource management**
a branch of archaeology that is concerned with developing policies and action in regard to the preservation and use of cultural resources.

■ **cultural resources**
materials or remains, including historic and archaeological objects, that compose a culture's non-renewable heritage. Also includes ethnographic objects, historic and prehistoric buildings, structures, sites and landscapes.

■ **culture history**
the identification and classification of cultural change through time. A primary aspect of archaeological interpretation concerned with es-

tablishing the chronological context of cultural items and complexes.

■ **culture sequence**
the chronological succession of cultural traits, phases or traditions in a local area.

■ **culture**
way of life, common beliefs and practices of a group of people. The integrated pattern of human knowledge, belief and behaviour that depends upon man's capacity for learning and transmitting knowledge to succeeding generations.

■ **culture-area**
a classification of cultures within a specific geographic-environmental region, sharing enough distinctive traits

to set them apart from the adjacent areas, e.g. Northwest Coast, Arctic, etc.

■ **culvert**
drainage- channel.

■ **curation agreement**
document/contract between two parties (one usually a repository) detailing the curation of a collection(s). It includes details on the state of the collection when given to the repository, work to be done at the repository, responsibilities to the collection for both parties, costs, ownership, and issues/details on access and use of the collection.

■ **curation**
the process of 'managing and preserving a collection according to professional museum and archival practices'.

■ **curator**

a trained professional who is usually responsible for the care, exhibition, research and enhancement of repository collections. Specific duties vary between repositories.

■ **curtain**

wall of fortification.

■ **custom**

established practice, habit, tradition.

■ **cutting blade**

(also 'end blade') the piercing element of a composite projectile point or harpoon head.

■ **dado**

continuous border round the lower part of a wall, decorated with painted plaster.

■ **dart**

a projectile point hafted to a shaft that utilised a throwing stick or atlatl or blowgun.

■ **dart point**

a flaked projectile point designed for use as a tip for a throwing stick dart.

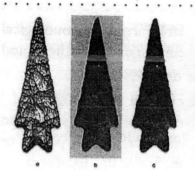

■ **datum plane**

an arbitrary or imaginary horizontal surface surveyed over a site from which vertical measurements are taken.

■ **datum**

a fixed reference point on an archaeological site from which measurements are taken.

■ **daub**

clay used to fill in the holes and gaps between the wood or thatching of a wall. It was used by both Indians and European settlers in north America to construct houses.

■ **deaccession**

the legal, permanent removal of an object, document, specimen or collection from a repository. Requires full documentation of the process.

## dead storage

method for storing objects that are not actively used. It usually involves less expensive, off-site facilities where collections are relatively inaccessible.

## debitage

debris remaining from the manufacturing of stone tools.

## deduction

a process of reasoning by which more specific consequences are inferred by rigorous argument from more general propositions.

## deductive nomological (d-n) explanation

a formal method of explanation, based on the testing of hypotheses derived from general laws.

## deed of gift

a contract that transfers ownership from one person or institution to another. Should include any conditions placed on the gift, although these are generally discouraged by the receiving repository.

## deep-sea cores

cores drilled from the sea bed that provide the most coherent record of climate changes on a worldwide scale. The cores contain shells of microscopic marine organisms (foraminifera) laid down on the ocean floor through the continuous process of sedimentation. Variations in the ratio of two oxygen isotopes in the calcium carbonate of these shells give a sensitive indicator of sea temperature at the time the organisms were alive.

## deity

a god.

■ **delamination**
the lateral separation of a surface into constituent layers.

■ **demography**
the study of the distribution, density and vital statistics of populations, as also the processes which contribute to population structure and their temporal and spatial dynamics.

■ **demotic**
an ancient Egyptian dialect.

■ **dendrochronology**
the scientific study of the annular growth of trees. Trees produce rings of various thicknesses annually, in response to rainfall. Tree-rings therefore, can be used to reconstruct fluctuations in rainfall in the past, reflecting past climatic conditions.

■ **dentalia**
small, slender horn-like Pacific Ocean shell used and traded as beads and wealth-items.

■ **dependent variable**
a variable that is affected b the independent variable.

■ **deposit**
any accumulation laid down by human occupational activities.

■ **derivative work**
variant or alternative version of an original piece of work such as posters, postcards, T-shirts or artwork, using original photographs, graphic designs, maps or the like.

■ **destructive analysis**
general term for any type of scientific analysis that destroys or alters the sample during the process. In archaeology, destructive analysis techniques include thin-section analysis, DNA analysis, C14 dating, thermo-luminescence dating and metallography.

■ **detritus**
waste by-products from tool manufacture. Most frequently applied to chips and

fragments resulting from stone flaking.

### ▪ devitrification

a change in the state of glass from a vitreous to a crystalline condition. It then loses its glassy lustre and transparency.

### ▪ devonian

a period of the Palaeozoic era, spanning the time between 410 and 360 million years ago. It is named after Devonshire, England, where rocks of this age were first studied.

### ▪ diachronic

referring to phenomena as they change over time, i.e. employing a chronological perspective.

### ▪ diagenesis

all chemical, physical and biological modifications undergone by a sediment after its initial deposition.

### ▪ diatom analysis

a method of environmental reconstruction based on plant microfossils. Diatoms are unicellular algae, whose silica cell walls survive after the algae die and they accumulate in large numbers at the bottom of rivers and lakes. Their assemblages directly reflect the floristic composition of the water's extinct communities, as well as the water's salinity, alkalinity and nutrient status.

### ▪ differential fluxgate magnetometer

a type of magnetometer used in subsurface detection, with the advantage of producing a continuous reading.

### ▪ diffusionist approach

the theory popularised by V.G. Childe that all the attributes of civilisation, from architecture to metalworking, had diffused from the Near East to Europe.

### ▪ dinocyst

a resting stage or reproductive stage in the life cycle of a dinoflagellate.

■ **dinoflagellate**

small organisms with both plant-like and animal-like characteristics, usually classified as algae (plants). They take their name from their twirling motion and their whip-like flagella.

■ **disposal**

the act of physically removing an object from a repository's collection.

■ **disposition schedule**

a policy document that directs how long a document (or type of document) is retained by an institution and whether it is permanently retained or may be discarded.

■ **disposition**

actions taken to records, deemed to not be current after appraisal. Actions include transfer to a records centre for temporary storage, transfer to an archival agency, donation to an eligible repository, reproduction on microfilm and destruction.

■ **distal end or tip**

that portion of a projectile, knife or other tool, or other hafted artefact which was designed for penetration, cutting or scraping. The end of the artefact that is farthest from the point of attachment, hafting or holding.

■ **distal**

that portion of a tool or bone which is farthest from the body of the user or 'owner'.

■ **disturbance**

a cultural deposit is said to be disturbed when the original sequence of deposition has been altered or upset by post-depositional factors. Agents of disturbance include natural forces such as stream or wind erosion, plant or animal activity, landslides, etc., and cultural forces such as later excavations.

■ **division of labour**

the set of rules found in all societies dictating how the day to day tasks are assigned to the various members of a society.

# DNA (deoxyribonucleic acid)

the material which carries the hereditary instructions (the 'blueprint') that determine the formation of all living organisms. Genes, the organisers of inheritance, are composed of DNA.

# double crib

two rooms or chambers connected by a single roof, to form a barn used for storage of grains or stabling of animals.

# dowsing

the supposed location of sub-surface features by employing a twig, copper rod, pendulum or other instrument. Discontinuous movements in these instruments are believed by some to record the existence of buried features.

# drift

a tool or implement, usually made of antler, which is used in the indirect percussion flaking process.

# driftless area

parts of NE Iowa, SE Minnesota and SW Wisconsin that weren't affected by the most recent ice age.

# drill

1. an oblong tool made of flaked stone, used in drilling holes in wood, leather or hides. Often at times, drills were made from well used projectile points, which were near end of life and thus many drills maintain the stem and hafting area of the original point type.

2. a tool used for perforating wood, bone and soft stone.

■ **drinking tube**
a length of hollow bird-bone used in aboriginal ceremonial situations for drinking liquids.

■ **drive-lanes**
aboriginal fences of rock piles or brush used to direct game-animals towards a trap.

■ **drumlin**
a streamlined hill or mound formed by a moving glacier, with the 'tail' in the direction of ice-flow.

■ **dry cleaning**
a technique to clean and remove contaminants off of documents, by gently brushing off surface grime and dirt by using 'Gummi' or 'Art Gum' erasers or by using archival 'groomsticks' to manually remove mould and other spores.

■ **early archaic**
a cultural period of the north American aborigine Indians, dating from 10,000 to 7,000 b.p.

■ **early man**
in the New World, this term refers to the oldest known human occupants - i.e. prior to ca. 8,000 b.p.

■ **ears**
pointed or rounded projections from the base or hafting area of certain projectile points.

■ **eastern cross timbers**
a relatively narrow, north-south strip of forested land that divides the Grand Prairie to the west from the Blackland Prairie to the east in North Central Texas. The Eastern Cross Timbers are associated with the sandier soils of the Woodbine geologic formation.

■ **echo-sounding**
an acoustic underwater-survey technique, used to trace the topography of submerged coastal plains and other buried land surfaces.

■ **ecofacts**
non-artefactual organic and environmental remains which have cultural relevance, e.g. faunal and floral material as well as soils and sediments.

# ■ ecological determinism

a form of explanation in which it is implicit that changes in the environment determine changes in human society.

# ■ ecology

the study of the dynamic relationships of organisms to each other and the total environment.

# ■ ecosystm

a group of organisms with specific relationships between themselves and a particular environment.

# ■ effigy

an object bearing the likeness of an animal or human.

# ■ effigy mound

an earthwork in the general shape of an animal (e.g. a snake, bird, etc.).

# ■ effigy pipe

an aboriginal smoking pipe shaped to resemble a human or animal form.

# ■ efflorescence

the outward migration and precipitation of salts on the surface, from within a porous material.

# ■ egalitarian society

a society that recognises few differences in wealth, power, prestige or status.

# ■ egyptologist

an archaeologist who specialises in the study of Ancient Egyptian culture and architecture.

# ■ electrical resistivity

see **soil resistivity.**

# ■ electrolysis

a standard cleaning process in archaeological conservation. Artefacts are placed in a chemical solution and by passing a weak current between them and a surrounding metal grill, the corrosive salts move from the cathode (object) to the anode (grill), removing any accumulated deposit and leaving the artefact clean.

# ■ electron probe microanalysis

used in the analysis of artefact composition, this technique is similar to XRF (X-ray fluorescence spectrometry) and is useful for studying small changes in composition within the body of an artefact.

# ■ Electron Spin Resonance (ESR)

a chronometric dating technique based upon the behaviour of electrons in crystals exposed to naturally occurring radioactivity. USR is used to date limestone, coral, shell, teeth and other materials. It enables trapped electrons within bone and shell to be measured without the heating that thermo-luminescence requires.

# ■ elevation

a measurement of vertical distance in mapping.

# ■ elliptical

1. a description of a projectile's cross section.

2. a cross section which looks like an ellipse, having two convex faces which taper near the blade edges.

# ■ empathetic method

the use of personal intuition (in German *Einfuhlung*) to seek to understand the inner lives of other people, using the assumption that there is a common structure to human experience. The assumption that the study of the inner experience of humans provides a handle for interpreting prehistory and history is made by idealist thinkers such as B. Croce, R.G. Collingwood and members of the 'postprocessual' school of thought.

# ■ empirical

received through the senses (sight, touch, smell, hearing, taste), either directly or through extensions.

# empiricism

reliance on observable and quantifiable data.

# emprassario system

a land grant system in the early Republic of Texas, in which four contracts were made to designate 'colonies' and bring immigrants to the Texas frontier. Contractors were to receive 10 sections of land for each 100 colonists introduced and up to half of the colonists' grants. Colonists were to receive grants similar in amount and requirements to fourth class headrights(a status issued to those who arrived to Texas between January 1, 1840 and January 1, 1842.), with the requirement of placing 15 acres into cultivation. The four colonies were Peters' Colony, Fisher and Miller's Colony, Mercer's Colony and Castro's Colony.

# emulation

one of the most frequent features accompanying competition, where customs, buildings and artefacts in one society may be adopted by neighbouring ones through a process of imitation which is often competitive in nature.

# end scraper

a stone tool formed by chipping the end of a flake of stone, which can then be used to scrape animal hides and wood.

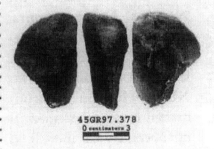

45GR97.378
0 centimeters 3

# engineer's level

an optical surveying instrument designed to obtain accurate level lines of sight and turn.

# engraving

the scratched lines into the surface of an object (i.e. pottery, slate, shell, metal).

# environmental archaeology

a field in which inter-disciplinary research, involving archaeologists and natural scientists, is directed at the reconstruction of human use of plants and animals and how past societies adapted to the changing environmental conditions.

# Environmental Assessment (EA)

a document related to the National Environmental Policy Act (NEPA) prepared by a Federal agency. Used for compliance with NEPA when an Environmental Impact Statement is not necessary, i.e., there is no significant impact.

# environmental circumscription

an explanation for the origins of the state, propounded by Robert Carneiro, that emphasises the fundamental role exerted by environmental constraints and by territorial limitations.

# Environmental Impact Statement (EIS)

a detailed statement prepared under compliance with the National Environmental Policy Act, which outlines the environmental impact of actions taken by a federal agency, as well as options for limiting or negating that impact.

# eocene

an epoch of the lower Tertiary period, spanning the time between 55.5 and 33.7 million years ago. Its name is from the Greek words 'eos' (dawn) and 'ceno' (new).

# eolian deposits

sediments transported by wind (e.g. sand-dunes, loess, etc.).

# eoliths

crude stone pebbles found in Lower Pleistocene contexts; once thought to be the work of human agency, but now generally regarded as natural products.

■ **erosion**

soil that is eaten away by water or wind.

■ **erratic**

a glacially transported boulder.

■ **esker**

a sinuous ridge of fluvial deposits resulting from a subglacial melt-water stream.

■ **estimation**

probable calculation or valuation.

■ **ethnicity**

a basis for social categories that are rooted in socially perceived differences in national origin, language, and/or religion.

■ **ethnocentrism**

the belief that one's culture is superior to all others.

■ **ethnographic analogy**

interpretation of archaeological remains by comparison to historical cultures.

■ **ethnography**

that aspect of cultural anthropology which is concerned with the descriptive documentation of living cultures.

■ **ethnohistory**

the study of ethnographic cultures through historical records.

■ **ethnology**

a subset of cultural anthropology concerned with the comparative study of contemporary cultures, with a view to deriving general principles about human society.

■ **ethnos**

the ethnic group, defined as a firm aggregate of people, historically established on a given territory, possessing, in common, relatively stable peculiarities of language and culture and also recognising their unity and difference as expressed in a self-contained group.

■ **excavated**
hollowed out cavity, explored.

■ **excavation grid**
a system of rectangular coordinates, established on the ground surface by stakes and string, which divides a site into excavation units.

■ **excavation**
digging up and removing artefacts and features from an archaeological site, in order to analyse and predict past human behaviour.

■ **excurvate**
a shape that bulges out in a graceful smooth convex curve. A term used to describe a convex blade edge or basal edge or stem.

■ **expanded or 'e' notched**
a notch type which is composed of two notches i close proximity that leave nipple as a remnant. Als known as a double notch.

■ **expanding**
generally, referring to th width of a stem or point tha is getting larger or wider.

■ **exposure**
1. a natural or artificial sec tion or cut into the grounc such as a wind blow-out, sea cliff or roadcut.
2. the orientation of a site ir relation to magnetic direc tion or the sun - e.g. a 'south ern exposure'.
3. the quality of colour, con trast and light in a photo graph.

■ **fabric**
1. a material woven of plan or animal fibres.
2. the orientation of sedi mentary particles.

# face

the broader area of a tool or projectile between the edges, this area could include the blade and hafting area.

# face, obverse

on a fluted projectile, it is the face from which the initial or primary flute was removed.

# face, reverse

on a fluted projectile, it is the face from which the secondary flute was removed.

# facility report

report prepared by a repository that outlines its facilities, environmental controls and monitoring and collections management procedures. Lending institutions often use these reports to decide whether a borrowing institution is able to properly care for and manage loaned objects.

# factor analysis

a multivariate statistical technique which assesses the degree of variation between artefact types and is based on a matrix of correlation coefficients which measure the relative association between any two variables.

# faience

glass-like material, first made in pre-dynastic Egypt. It involves coating a core material of powdered quartz with a vitreous alkaline glaze.

# fall-off analysis

the study of regularities in the way in which quantities of traded items found in the archaeological record decline as the distance from the source increases. This may be plotted as a falloff curve, with the quantities of material (Y-axis) plotted against distance from source (X-axis).

# ■ fantasy

stories set in an unreal world. Fantasy is based upon the imagination in one's mind.

# ■ farming

act of growing crops on the land.

# ■ fauna

a Latin term which refers to animal remains, as opposed to flora which refers to plant remains.

# ■ faunal dating

a method of relative dating based on observing the evolutionary changes in particular species of mammals, so as to form a rough chronological sequence.

# ■ faunal remains

bones and other animal parts found in archaeological sites are important in the reconstruction of past ecosystem and cultural subsistence patterns.

# ■ features

evidence of human activities at a site which are visible as disturbances in the soil. Some examples of such disturbances are: digging pits for storage, setting posts for houses in the form of post moulds or by constructing a hearth for cooking. These disturbances are often distinguished by soil discolouration or non-natural formations of stone, shell, bone, soil, coals, wood, etc.

# ■ field data forms

printed forms used to record archaeological survey or excavation information. Special forms are frequently used to record artefact proveniences, features and burials, site locations and descriptions and level-notes.

# ■ field walk

process by which surface artefacts can be discovered before excavation occurs. This is a useful step in determining the potential of an archaeological site.

# ■ field-system

regular pattern of rectangular fields attached to an ancient farming settlement.

# ■ filigree

fine open metalwork using wires and soldering, first developed in the Near East.

# ■ finding aid

1. a broader term for any format of textual or electronic tool that assists researchers in locating or using archival and manuscript collections. Basic finding aids include guides, e.g. repository, collection and subject guides, descriptive inventories, accession registers, card catalogues, special lists, e.g. shelf and box lists, indexes and for machine-readable records, software documentation.

2. the file guides, indexes, registers and filing system aids produced by the records creator, usually referred to as 'control records' or 'contemporaneous finding aids'.

3. the specific type of descriptive tool described in the text above.

# ■ fire-cracked rock (f.c.r.)

'fire-broken rock'. Rocks cracked or broken by the heat of a fire, a common element in aboriginal campsite debris.

■ **fishing station**

a special type of site located on streams, lakes or ocean beaches, where fishing activities were carried on. May be characterised by a fish-trap or WEIR.

■ **flagging**

or 'survey tape', a brightly coloured plastic ribbon used to mark features, sites, surveyed stakes, etc., to aid in their relocation.

■ **flake scar**

1. a scar that remains on a flaked artefact resulting from the removal of a flake during the manufacture of the artefact.
2. the negative area left on a stone core or nucleus, after the removal of a conchoidal flake.

■ **flake**

a thin flat asymmetrical fragment of flint or other stone intentionally removed from a core or nucleus of cryptocrystalline or fine-grained rock by percussion or pressure. May be used as a tool with no further deliberate modification, may be retouched or may serve as a preform for further reduction.

■ **flaking**

the removal of flakes during the manufacture of a flaked artefact. Baton flaking is the term used to describe the removal of flakes from stone by striking blows with a baton-like tool, a method of direct percussion flaking.

■ **flaking alternate biface bevel**

Where the opposite face of each edge is steeply flaked and each face opposing the bevelled edge is flatly flaked.

# ■ flaking station

a specialised site or activity area within a site, dominated by evidence for the past manufacture of flaked stone artefacts. Might consist of an area of concentrated detritus, cores, flaking-tools and preforms.

# ■ flaking tool

a tool, such as an antler billet or antler drift, which was used in removing flakes during the manufacture of a flaked stone projectile, tool, blade or artefact.

# ■ flaking, baseward

the removal of flakes from the distal tip at a downward angle towards the basal edge.

# ■ flaking, benton

this flaking technique involved the removal of large and small percussion flakes which resulted in numerous step fractures. Pressure flaking was often used to form serrations. Oblique-transverse flaking was used to shape the blade of a few examples.

# ■ flaking, biface bevel

this flaking technique involved the removal of elongate, steep, pressure or percussion flakes just opposite each other, from an edge, to form a biface bevel and often biface serrations.

# ■ flaking, biface serration

this flaking technique involved the removal of elongate, not so steep, pressure or percussion flakes just opposite each other, from an edge, to form biface serrations.

# ■ flaking, chevron

a v-shaped flaking pattern which extended beyond the distal tip along much or all of one or both faces of a blade.

# ■ flaking, early archaic percussion-pressure

a type of flaking in which the preform was shaped by percussion flaking. The blade edges were ground to prepare a surface for the removal of elongate pressure flakes. The pressure flaking may have taken the form of alternate uniface bevel flaking, biface serration flaking, alternate biface bevel flaking or irregular pressure flaking.

**■ flaking, flat**
the removal of thin flakes by striking the artefact at a small angle to the plane of the face.

**■ flaking, flint creek**
a characteristic flaking style of the flint creek culture which was accomplished by removing regular, deep, elongate, opposing pressure flakes from the blade edges. The application of this flaking style usually resulted in the formation of very fine biface serrations.

**■ flaking, horizontal transverse**
a unique flaking style where horizontal parallel flakes are removed that extend from one edge of the blade, acro to the other edge.

**■ flaking, oblique transverse**
a unique flaking style in whic the removal of flakes from blade face results in long d agonal parallel flake sca which extend from one sid of the blade across the blad face to the other side of th blade.

**■ flaking, opposing**
flakes were struck just oppo site each other from oppos ing faces.

**■ flaking, opposing pressure**
in finishing blade edges pressure flakes were re moved from each face oppo site of each other.

**■ flaking, parallel (a.k.a. collateral flaking).**
a secondary flaking technique that is often found on the earliest projectile points and stone tools, usually performed on the blade faces, in

which the removal of flakes was performed in such a manner so as to remove flakes of similar size, depth, length and direction, to result in flake scars which are parallel. Typically, the mark of a well accomplished flint knapper. Such flake scars are found only on few specimens and can be quite aesthetically beautiful to behold.

■ **flaking, percussion**
a flaking technique which involved the striking of a preform with a billet, a hammer stone or other flaking tool. This flaking technique usually left a hinge or step fracture.

■ **flaking, pressure**
a flaking technique which involved the removal of flakes by pressure against the edge of a preform with a pointed implement or flaking tool such as bone or antler.

■ **flaking, primary**
initial flaking, usually broad, shallow, random percussion,

used to roughly shape a preform into a desired outline for a tool or projectile.

■ **flaking, random**
the removal of flakes with no regard to the resulting aesthetic alignment of flake scars.

■ **flaking, regular**
the removal of closely aligned flakes of similar lengths and widths which result in an aesthetically pleasing flake scar design.

■ **flaking, secondary**
following the primary flaking, this flaking technique was applied to remove medium-sised pressure or percussion flakes in shaping the blade and basal edges, forming notches or producing serrations.

■ **flaking-tool (also 'flaker')**
any implement used to remove conchoidal flakes by percussion or pressure from a nucleus of suitable mate-

rial. May be a pointed antler or bone pressure-flaking tool or a small hammer-stone used for percussion.

# ■ flesher

a toothed implement manufactured on an animal long-bone, used for scraping hides.

# ■ flexed burial

1. a body that is buried in the foetal position.
2. a human interment where the body is placed in a semi-foetal position, with the knees drawn up against the chest and hands near the chin.

# ■ flint

a quartz with a high silica content that produces a conchoidal fracture when chipped, it is usually found in association with chalk, limestone and other rock deposits which contain lime. It commonly occurs in small ovoid nodules as well as in larger veins. Impure flint is known as chert, which varies widely as t texture, colour, grain an knapping characteristic Pure flint is so hard an even-grained that it wa used by early man as a vit necessity in producin spear point, dart poin knives and other utilitaria tools. Late stone-age ma learned that when struc with a high iron conten rock, the flint gave of sparks. Thus, flint becam iron-age man's method o producing fire. Flint come in many colours from whit to black, including grey tan, brown, olive, blue an other variants and mottle combinations.

# ■ flint knappers

humans that flake stone, sucl as flint, into projectiles and tools or replicas thereof.

■ **flint**

a microcrystalline silicate rock, similar to chert, used for the manufacture of flaked stone tools. Colour most commonly grey, honey-brown or black.

■ **floor-plan**

a scale drawing of features, matrix changes and important associations completed for the end of each excavation level.

■ **flora**

plants of a given region or period of geologic time.

■ **floral remains**

remnants of past vegetation found in archaeological sites useful in the reconstruction of past environments.

■ **flotation**

the process of recovering small particles of organic material by immersing sediment samples in water or other fluids and skimming off the particles which float on the surface. It is an important method for obtaining micro-floral and micro-faunal remains and carbon samples, seeds, e.g. small bones and other relevant organic materials from the soil of a site.

■ **flue-arch**

under-floor arch in a hypocaust, allowing hot air to pass from furnace to room or from one heated room to another.

■ **flue-tiles**

open-ended, box-shaped tiles built in the thickness of the walls of a room heated by hypocaust.

■ **flute**

a long narrow grove, resulting from the removal of an elongated channel flake, which extends from the basal edge of a projectile for some distance along the face, used to thin the hafting area.

■ **flute, median**

on multi-fluted faces, it is the main, the central most and usually the longest flute.

■ **flute, primary**

the first median flute to be removed in the fluting process.

■ **flute, secondary**

the second median flute to be removed in the fluting process. This flute was removed from the face opposite the primary flute.

■ **flute**

a long, narrow flake removed from a spear point to aid in the binding of the point to the spear shaft.

■ **fluted**

grooved or channelled. A fluted point is a projectile point that has had one or more flutes, i.e. long thinning flakes removed from the base along one or both faces, e.g. Clovis or Folsom points.

■ **flutes, lateral**

the initial, usually short flutes, that were removed from either side of the mid-portion of the basal edge to form a

striking platform for the re moval of the median flute.

■ **fluting, multiple**

a technique of fluting that in volved the removal of two short lateral flutes, in prepa ration for the removal of a longer flute.

■ **fluting, single**

projectiles or tools which have one flute per face.

■ **fluvial deposits**

sediments laid down by run ning water.

■ **focus**

synonymous with phase.

■ **folsom point**

large stone projectile point used by early American hunt ers to kill large game animals.

■ **foraging**

collecting wild plants and hunting wild animals for sub sistence.

■ **foraminifer**

protozoans that belong to the subclass Sarcodina, order Foraminifera, that have a test of one to many chambers composed of secreted calcite or agglutinated particles.

## ■ foreshaft

a separate, often detachable piece, between the point and main shaft of a projectile.

## ■ formation processes

those processes affecting the way in which archaeological materials came to be buried and their subsequent history afterwards. Cultural formation processes include the deliberate or accidental activities of humans. Natural formation processes refer to natural or environmental events that govern the burial and survival of the archaeological record.

## ■ fossil beach

'paleo-beach', 'raised beach', 'fossil strandline'. A lake or ocean beach developed when the water-level was significantly different from that of the present. Most commonly, these will be 'raised beaches' or old strandline

features and sediments found above the modern shoreline.

## ■ fossil cuticles

the outermost protective layer of the skin of leaves or blades of grass, made of cutin, a very resistant material that survives in the archaeological record often in faeces. Cuticular analysis is a useful adjunct to palynology in environmental reconstruction.

## ■ fossil ice wedges

soil features caused when the ground freezes and contracts, opening up fissures in the permafrost that fill with wedges of ice. The fossil wedges are proof of past cooling of climate and of the depth of permafrost.

# fossil

fossils are the recognisable remains, such as bones, shells or leaves or other evidence, such as tracks, burrows or impressions, of past life on Earth.

# fossilisation

all the processes that involve the burial of a plant or animal in sediment and the eventual preservation of all, part or a trace of it.

# fracture, hinge

a recurvate upstep where the distal end of a blade or flake abruptly broke from the parent material. Such a flake scar is indicative of a cruder form of percussion flaking.

# fracture, impact

a breakage of the distal tip of a projectile, which is characterised by a missing portion of the tip and an elongate fracture scar extending along one face of the blade. Usually occurring during impact when a point was thrown or shot.

# fracture, step

a vertical upstep where the distal end of a blade or flake broke from the parent material. Such a flake scar is indicative of a well-executed percussion flaking.

# frequency seriation

a relative dating method which relies principally on measuring changes in the proportional abundance or frequency, observed among finds (e.g. counts of tool types or of ceramic fabrics).

# frieze

horizontal band above an architrave, sometimes carved with sculpture.

■ **frigidarium**
cold room in a bath-suite.

■ **functionalism**
the theory that all elements of a culture are functional in that they serve to satisfy culturally defined needs of the people in that society or requirements of the society as a whole.

■ **functional-processual approach**
see **processual archaeology**.

■ **funerary objects**
items that, as part of the death rite or ceremony of a culture, are reasonably believed to have been placed intentionally with or near individual human remains at the time of death or later. Used in NAGPRA.

■ **genes**
the basic units of inheritance, now known to be governed by the specific sequence of the genetic markers within the DNA of the individual concerned.

■ **genre**
refers to the document's style, content and form, including the document's purpose (advertisements, presentation album), the document's viewpoint (panoramic view), broad topical category (landscape, still life, portrait or street scene), method of representation (abstract, figurative), circumstances of creation (amateur works, student works) or function (dance cards, cigarette cards, death certificates).

■ **geochemical analysis**
the investigation technique which involves taking soil samples at regular intervals from the surface of a site and measuring their phosphate content and other chemical properties.

■ **geochemistry**
the science that deals with chemical changes in and the

composition of the earth's crust.

# ■ geochronology

aging of artefacts based on the age of the geological formations in which they are located.

# ■ geographic coordinates

the world-wide system of latitude and longitude, used to define the location of any point on the earth's surface.

# ■ Geographic Information System (GIS)

computer system capable of assembling, storing, manipulating and displaying geographically referenced information (data identified according to its location). GIS is often used in archaeology for making maps that plot artefact distribution over a site or sites, over a geographic area. Requires extensive data gathering and sophisticated software.

# ■ geography

the study of the earth's surface and its contours.

# ■ geologic time scale

an arbitrary chronological sequence of geologic events, used as a measure of the age of any part of geologic time, usually presented in the form of a chart showing the names of the various rock-stratigraphic time-stratigraphic or geologic-time units.

# ■ geologic time

the period of time extending from the formation of the earth to the present.

# ■ geologist

a person who studies the history of the earth and its life, especially as recorded in rocks.

# ■ geology

study of the minerals and rocks making up the crust of the earth.

# ■ geo-magnetic reversals

an aspect of archaeomagnetism relevant to the dating of the Lower Paleolithic, involving complete reversals in the earth's magnetic field.

## geomorphology

a sub-discipline of geography, concerned with the study of the form and development of the landscape, it includes such specialisations as sedimentology.

## georadar

a technique used in ground reconnaissance, similar to soil-sounding radar, but with a much larger antenna and more extensive coverage.

## gift exchange

see **reciprocity**.

## glacial lake

a lake formed of ponded glacial meltwater or by the damming of a drainage system by glacial activity. A 'pro-glacial' lake has at least one margin formed by glacial ice.

## glacial maximum

the position and period of greatest advance of a glacier.

## glacial striae

scratches on bedrock or loose stones caused by glacial abrasion. May be large or microscopic and could, in some cases, be mistaken for evidence of human activity.

## glacial

a period of expansion of glacial ice.

## glottochronology

a controversial method of assessing the temporal divergence of two languages, based on changes of vocabulary (lexicostatistics) and expressed as an arithmetic formula.

## gorge (also 'gorge-hook')

a bone bipoint used to catch fish or waterfowl. After being swallowed, the hook will toggle in the stomach of the prey and cannot be drawn out.

# gorget

a ornament made of stone, slate or shell which was typically ground, drilled with one or more holes and polished. These artefacts were presumably worn over the chest or around the throat and were either suspended on a cord or attached directly to clothing. Another possible use of the gorget was as an atlatl weight.

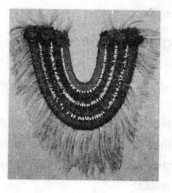

# graffito

writing scratched on tile, pottery, plaster, etc.

# granulation

the soldering of grains of metal to a background, usually of the same metal and much used by the Etruscans.

# grave goods

also 'grave inclusions', 'mortuary goods', etc., tools, weapons, food or ceremonial objects placed with a burial, meant to equip the person for the after life.

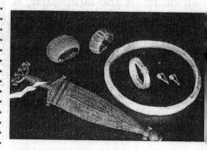

# graver

a small pointed or chisel-like stone tool with a sharp tip, used to engrave bone, stone, wood or other materials.

# grey literature

unpublished documentation that is printed in limited numbers and is rarely catalogued in libraries. For archaeology, it is mainly technical reports of archaeological investigations that are most often associated with cultural resources management, assessment and fieldwork. Thus, it is relatively inaccessible to researchers, other archaeologists and the public.

# grid-system

a system of rectangular excavation or sampling units laid over a site by strings and stakes.

# grinding

a method of stone working employed in the smoothing of an edge or surface by rubbing it with a hammerstone or other abrader, prior to use. Performed on projectiles or blades so that hafting materials (lashings) would not be cut by sharp edges of the base. Also commonly referred to as basal grinding when the base and sides of the stem have been ground. There are varying degrees of grinding, typically referred to as light, moderate or heavy.

# grit

crushed stone or sand placed in clay in order to make potter vessels stronger.

# grit and grog tempered pottery

sand (grit) and crushed pottery sherds (grog) mixed in the unfired clay to make ceramic vessels stronger. These inclusions prevented the rapid expansion of the paste as the clay's water content was boiled away when the pottery was fired.

# grit

crushed stone or sand placed in clay in order to make potter vessels stronger.

# ground

an edge or surface that was smoothed by abrasion.

# ground reconnaissance

a collective name for a wide variety of methods, for identifying individual archaeological sites, including consultation of documentary sources, place-name evidence, local folklore and legend, but primarily actual fieldwork.

■ **ground stone**

stone artefacts shaped by sawing, grinding, and/or polishing with abrasive materials, e.g. 'ground slate knives', 'polished soapstone pendants', etc.

■ **guilloche**

on mosaics, decorative feature consisting of two or more intertwining bands of herringbone. Descriptive of a style of construction in which stonework or tiles are set in zig-zag pattern.

■ **gun-flint**

a square blade-segment of flint used to ignite the powder charge of a flint-lock gun. Often mistaken for an aboriginal artefact.

■ **habitation area**

a generalised term for a house or tent floor or the remains of any other type of aboriginal shelter.

■ **habitation site**

a location where a human group has lived and conducted normal daily activities for a significant period.

■ **hadean**

the earliest subdivision of the Precambrian, spanning the time between the formation of the Earth, about 4.5 billion years ago and the start of the Archaean era, 3.8 billion years ago. This interval predates the period of true geologic time since no rocks of this age are known on Earth, with the exception of a few meteorites.

# haft

to attach a shaft or handle to a projectile or knife blade.

# hafted

attached with a binding to a shaft or handle e.g. a 'hafted knife'.

# hafting area

the basal portion or proximal end of a projectile or knife blade which was designed for attaching or lashing or adhering to a shaft or handle for use. The characteristics of this portion of a projectile/blade artefact are critical for accurate identification. Such attributes as notching, fluting, thinning, grinding or stemming are key diagnostic elements for point typology. In most cases, a specimen can be classified if only this portion of the example is found intact, while the absence of this part will make a specific analysis and typology effort difficult or impossible.

# haiku

brief poem of seventeen syllables.

# half-life

the time taken for half the quantity of a radioactive isotope in a sample to decay (see also radioactive decay).

# hammerstone

a stone, usually a natural rounded hard largely unmodified river pebble that shows battering scars resulting from repeated use as an unhafted hammer or platform in the flaking process.

# hand-axe

a Palaeolithic stone tool usually made by modifying (chipping or flaking) a natural pebble.

■ **hand-level**

a small, simple, hand-held surveying instrument for establishing horizontal lines-of-sight over short distances.

■ **hand-maul**

a carefully manufactured unhafted stone hammer.

■ **hard-hammer percussion**

a crude flint-knapping technique used to break down large rocks by striking one against the other.

■ **harpoon head (point)**

the arming tip of a harpoon, generally classifiable into 2 main forms - toggling and barbed - each of which may be composite or single-piece and may or may not carry additional cutting-blades or side-blades. Always have line-guards or other means of line attachment.

■ **harpoon**

a thrown or thrust spear-like weapon armed with a detachable point fastened to a retrieving line.

■ **hauterivian**

European stage of the Lower Cretaceous, spanning the time between 122 and 118 million years ago.

■ **hearth**

a fireplace, often circular and may be unlined, rock or clay-lined or rock-filled.

■ **heat treating**

the use of fire to heat and thermally alter a stone 'preform', in an attempt to improve its working characteristics and flaking qualities prior to knapping and flaking. Typical result of heat treating is a colour change of the stone as well as the molecular structure. Heat treating occurs at temperatures that approximate or exceed 350 degrees centigrade.

■ **heat treatment**

an aboriginal process by which the flaking properties

of a rock were improved by controlled heating in a fire.

## hegemony

preponderant influence or authority of one individual or social group over another.

## heliocentric

a sun-centred model of the universe.

## hematite

a natural iron oxide which was used as a reddish pigment.

## henge

literally, 'hanging rock', this term is often applied to the Neolithic stone monoliths found in Britian.

## herd

among geladas, a large social unit consisting of several bands that come together under very good grazing conditions.

## hermeneutics

formal study of methods of interpretation. Following Gadamer, the hermeneutical process is often regarded as involving complex interaction between the interpreting subject and the interpreted object.

## hewn

wood shaped by heavy cutting or chopping blows struck by hand tools such as axes or adzes.

## hide scraper

a tool made out of bone or stone used for removing the flesh from an animal hide.

## hieroglyphs

the pictographic symbols of ancient writing systems.

## hinge fracture

1. a scar left behind when the terminal end of a blade or flake, being struck from the parent material, makes a sharp dip into the material causing a deep abrupt fracture.

2. weak or inward-directed blow against crypto-crystalline or fine-grained rock will produce a flake which breaks off or 'hinges' halfway along,

without carrying through to a thin tapered end.

■ **historic**
a cultural period of the north American aborigine Indians, dating from 450 to 170 b.p.

■ **historic period**
the time after European contact or the beginning of written recording.

■ **historic preservation**
management and preservation of buildings, sites, structures, objects and landscapes that have historical or cultural significance.

■ **historic sites act of 1935**
public law 74-292; 49 statute 666 enabling the authorised expenditure of funds for archaeological studies on major land modification projects.

■ **historical archaeology**
the archaeological study of historically documented cultures. In North America, research is directed at colonial and post-colonial settlement, analogous to the study of medieval and post-medieval archaeology in Europe.

■ **historical particularism**
a detailed descriptive approach to anthropology, associated with Franz Boas and his students and designed as an alternative to the broad generalising approach favoured by anthropologists such as Morgan and Tylor.

■ **historiographic approach**
a form of explanation based primarily on traditional descriptive historical frameworks.

■ **hoards**
deliberately buried groups of valuables or prised possessions, often in times of conflict or war and which, for one reason or another, have not been reclaimed. Metal hoards are a primary source of evidence for the European Bronze Age.

# holism

the philosophical view that no complex entity can be considered to be only the sum of its parts. As a principle of anthropology, the assumption that any given aspect of human life is to be studied with an eye to its relation to other aspects of human life.

# holocene

an epoch of the Quaternary period, spanning the time from the end of the Pleistocene (8,000 years ago) to the present. It is named after the Greek words 'holos' (entire) and 'ceno' (new).

# holotype

among the primary types, a holotype is the original specimen selected as the type and from which the original description for the type or the original illustration, i.e. photograph, was made.

# homeostasis

a term used in systems thinking to describe the action of negative feedback processes in maintaining the system at a constant equilibrium state.

# homotype

a homotype is a specimen not used in the literature but identified by a specialist, after analysis and comparison with the attributes of a holotype.

# Hopewellian/Hopewell

refers to a prehistoric culture from Ohio, known for elaborate burial practices.

# horizon

1. a discrete regional cultural period or level of cultural development marked by a group of some easily recognisable criteria or traits with a wide geographical distribution and a brief duration.
2. in soil-science terminology, a natural developmental zone in a soil profile such as the 'A-horizon'.

# horizontal angle

in mapping, the angle of sight measured on the level or horizontal plane.

■ **horizontal circle**

with major surveying instruments, the graduated horizontal table around which the sighting telescope revolves. It is used to measure the horizontal angle.

■ **horizontal datum**

a base measuring point ('0.0 point') used as the origin of rectangular coordinate systems for mapping or for maintaining excavation provenience.

■ **horizontal distance**

the measurement of distance on a true level plane.

■ **horizontal provenience**

the location of an object on a two-dimensional plane surface.

■ **horticulture**

1.the science and art of growing fruit, flowers, ornamental plants and vegetables in small gardens.
2.plant cultivation carried out with relatively simple tools and methods.

■ **household**

a domestic residential group whose members live together in intimate contact, rear children, share the proceeds of labour and other resources held in common and in general cooperate on a day-to-day basis.

■ **house-pit**

an aboriginally excavated house floor.

■ **human relations area files**

a compilation of reports on 330 societies that are used for cross-cultural research.

■ **humectant**

a hygroscopic chemical that bonds to organic materials, thereby blocking the sites in the material that normally absorb and lose water. When the relative humidity (RH) drops, water is 'taken' by the object from the humectant. Common humectants are glycerol and sorbitol.

■ **humerus**

the large upper arm bone.

■ **humidification**

application of small amounts of moisture in an enclosed humidification chamber to relax paper fibres, so that a document can be gently unrolled or unfolded and then flattened.

■ **hunter-gatherers**

a collective term for the members of small-scale mobile or semi-sedentary societies, whose subsistence is mainly focused on hunting game and gathering wild plants and fruits. Organisational structure is based on bands with strong kinship ties.

■ **hunting and gathering**

involves the systematic collection of vegetable foods, hunting of game and fishing.

■ **hydrogeology**

the science that deals with subsurface waters and geologic aspects of surface waters.

■ **hygrothermograph**

device used to measure and record relative humidity (RH) and temperature levels in one area, over a continuous period. Depending on the machine, it can record levels for one day, one week or one month.

■ **hypocaust**

Roman method of central heating: The floor was raised, usually on pilae and flue-tiles acting as 'chimneys' were built in the thickness of the walls. The draught created by these flues enabled hot air to be drawn from the stoke-hole on the right in, where brushwood or other fuel was burnt, to circulate under the floor and to escape up the wall-flues to the air outside. In the channelled type of hypocaust, the hot air circulated not around pilae but through narrow channels built under the floor.

# hypothesis

a statement that stipulates a relationship between a phenomenon for which the researcher seeks to account and one or more other phenomena.

# hypothetico-deductive explanation

a form of explanation based on the formulation of hypothesis and the establishment from them by deduction of consequences which can then be tested against the archaeological data.

# ice cores

borings taken from the Arctic and Antarctic polar ice caps, containing layers of compacted ice useful for the reconstruction of palaeoenvironments and as a method of absolute dating.

# ice-wedge

a vertical wedge-shaped vein of ground ice found in permafrost areas. Causes 'polygonal ground' and may result in severe disturbance o archaeological sites.

# iconography

an important component o cognitive archaeology, thi involves the study of artisti representations which usu ally have an overt religious o ceremonial significance, e.g individual deities may be dis tinguished, each with a spe cial characteristic, such a corn with the corn god or the sun with a sun goddess, etc.

# idealist explanation

a form of explanation tha lays great stress on the search for insights into the historical circumstances, leading up to the event under study in terms primarily of the idea and motives of the individuals involved.

# imbrex

semi-circular roofing-tile, linking two flat tiles (tegulae).

# impact fracture

see fracture, impact

■ **in perpetuity**

literally means continuing forever. Used in reference to the curation of material remains and documents by a repository for the entire length of an item's life.

■ **in situ**

1. Latin expression meaning 'in its original position'.
2. archaeological items are said to be 'in situ' when they are found in the location where they were last deposited. In archeology, it references the original burial context or provenience of an object.

■ **incised**

a decoration found on pottery consisting of lines drawn into wet clay. When fired, the arrangement of lines leaves a permanent design on the vessel surface.

■ **inclined sights**

in mapping, a vertically angled line of sight.

■ **inclusion**

1. a foreign solid which is enclosed in the mass of an otherwise homogeneous mineral or material.
2. an intentional cultural association, such as gravegoods with a burial.

■ **increment borer**

a hand-operated coring device for obtaining tree-ring samples.

■ **incurvate**

a term to describe the outline or shape that is indented or convex, a form of basal edge or stem base outline.

■ **independent variable**

the variable that can cause change in other variables.

■ **index**

a spirit-bubble levelling device on the vertical circle of major surveying instruments.

■ **indirect percussion**

a technique for flaking stone artefacts by interposing a bone or antler punch between the hammer and the raw materials. Allows greater control than direct percussion flaking.

### ■ induction

a method of reasoning in which one proceeds by generalisation from a series of specific observations so as to derive general conclusions.

### ■ Inductively Coupled Plasma Emission Spectrometry (ICPS)

based on the same basic principles as OES (optical emission spectrometry), but the generation of much higher temperatures reduces problems of interference and produces more accurate results.

### ■ industry

all the artefacts in a site that are made from the same material, such as the bone industry.

### ■ information management

the development and maintenance of integrated infor-

mation systems and th optimisation of informatio flow and access. In reposito ries, this most often applie to the systems (manual o computerised) that hold col lections information. Thi may include accession, cata logue and/or inventory records.

### ■ Infrared Absorption Spectroscopy

a technique used in the characterisation of raw materials it has been particularly useful in distinguishing amber from different sources: the organic compounds in the amber absorb different wavelengths of infrared radiation passed through them.

### ■ innovation

the process of adopting a new thing, idea or behaviour pattern into a culture.

### ■ institutions

a society's recurrent patterns of activity, such as religion, art, a kinship system, law and family life.

## instrument height

the elevation of the line-of-sight of a surveying instrument above the immediate ground surface.

## instrument position (ip)

the location at which a surveying instrument is established to obtain a sighting.

## instrument

a general term for major optical surveying equipment, including transits, alidades and surveyor's levels.

## intellectual rights/ intellectual property rights

non-physical (intangible) rights to an object or record that exist independently from the ownership of the physical item. They include copyrights, images and rights to use.

## intensification

an increase in the product derived from a unit of land or labour.

## intensive agriculture

a form of agriculture that involves the use of draft animals or tractors, ploughs and often some form of irrigation.

## interaction sphere

this term refers to prehistoric groups who shared social interaction and exchanged materials or finished goods, through a network made up of medium to long distance trade contacts, e.g. the Hopewell interaction sphere.

## interglacial

a period of warming between two glacials.

## intermediate directions

northeast, northwest, southeast, southwest.

## intervention/

## interventive materials

materials, such as consolidants, fumigants, acids and other chemicals, used for the treatment of objects and records, including the addition of preservatives or the removal of agents of deterioration.

## interview

a record of a conversation between an interviewer and a subject. The intent of the interviewer is to provide for the readers an overview and understanding of the subject being interviewed.

## invention

any new thing, idea or way of behaving that emerges from within a society.

## inventory

an itemised listing of objects in a repository. It may also be the process of physically locating objects through several different types of inventory: complete, sectional and spot.

## iron age

a cultural stage characterised by the use of iron as the main metal.

## isostatic uplift

rise in the level of the land relative to the sea, caused by the relaxation of Ice Age conditions. It occurs when the weight of ice is removed as temperatures rise and the landscape is raised up to form raised beaches.

## isotopic analysis

an important source of information on the reconstruction of prehistoric diets, this technique analyses the ratios of the principal isotopes preserved in human bone. In effect, the method reads the chemical signatures left in the body by different foods. Isotopic analysis is also used in characterisation studies.

## isotopic dating

radiometric dating. All methods of age determination based on nuclear decay of naturally occurring radioactive isotopes. Age in years for geologic materials are calculated by measuring the presence of a short-life radioactive element, e.g. carbon-14 or by measuring the presence of a long-life radioactive element plus its decay product, e.g. potassium-40/argon-40.

# jamb

side-post of a doorway or window.

# Japanese paper

non-technical term for a type of archival quality, non-wood pulp paper that is often used in museum applications.

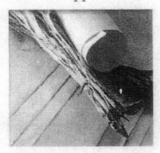

# jasper

a colloquial term for some varieties of chert. Usually refers to dark red or dull-green, fine-grained, semi-translucent banded materials used in point production.

# Jurassic

the middle period of the Mesozoic era, spanning the time between 213 and 145 million years ago. It is named after the Jura Mountains between France and Switzerland, where rocks of this age were first studied.

# kill-site

a type of special activity site where large game animals were killed and butchered.

# knife

a tool which was flaked to form one or more elongate cutting edges.

# knobbed

a stem form having a rounded lump or protruding appearance.

■ **kula ring**

a system of ceremonial, non-competitive, exchange practiced in Melanesia to establish and reinforce alliances. Malinowski's study of this system was influential in shaping the anthropological concept of reciprocity.

■ **labret**

a 'cuff-link' or pulley-shaped object of stone, bone or wood, inserted in a perforation of the lower lip as an ornament or status symbol by some aboriginal peoples.

■ **laconicum**

hot room, i.e. one with dry heat in a bath-suite.

■ **lacustrine deposits**

lake sediments, usually fine laminated silts and clays.

■ **laminae**

very thin strata.

■ **lanceolate**

shaped like the head of a lance or leaves, narrow and tapered toward the distal end and sometimes towards both ends. A term used to describe a major projectile point form that has no notches or shoulders or definable stem. Bases can be round, straight, concave, convex. A sub-type form of lanceolate could be lanceolate-triangular.

■ **landsat**

see **remote sensing**.

■ **landscape archaeology**

the study of individual features including settlements.

■ **late archaic**

a cultural period of the north American aborigine Indians dating from 4,000 to 3,000 b.p.

■ **late paleo**

a cultural period of the north American aborigine Indians

dating from 15,000 to 10,000 b.p.

**■ late woodland**

a cultural period of the north American aborigine Indians dating from 1,300 to 400 b.p. also known as Mississippian.

**■ latrine**

lavatory.

**■ leaching**

a natural process by which chemicals and minerals are transported downwards through a soil-profile.

**■ legal subdivision system**

the method of describing parcels of land in terms of 'Township, Range, Section and Quarter Section'.

**■ legend**

a story handed down from earlier times.

**■ leister**

a composite fishing spear made up of barbed side-pieces surrounding an unbarbed central point.

**■ length-width ratio**

the ratio of greatest length over the greatest width.

**■ lenticular**

a term used to describe a cross section of a blade that is excurvate on both faces, thus looking like a convex lens or an ellipse. Sometimes also referred to as elliptical.

**■ level bag**

a bag containing excavated materials from a single level of a single excavation unit.

**■ level notes**

written observations on all significant characteristics of an excavated level.

**■ level**

the basic vertical subdivision of an excavation unit. May

be natural, arbitrary or contoured.

# lexicostatistics

the study of linguistic divergence between two languages, based on changes in a list of common vocabulary terms and the sharing of common root words.

# lichenometry

the study of lichen growth as an aid to dating surface rock features and rock art.

# life expectancy

the length of time that a person can, on an average, expect to live.

# light-table

a glass-topped table illuminated from underneath, used in the laboratory photography of archaeological specimens.

# lignite

a soft shiny black variety of coal, aboriginally used to manufacture decorative objects.

# lineage

a unilineal descent group composed of people who trace their genealogies through specified links to a common ancestor.

# lineal descendant

individual tracing his or her ancestry directly and without interruption through the traditional kinship system of his/her group to a known individual. Used in compliance with NAGPRA, the lineal descendant has priority claim over human remains or funerary/sacred objects of his/her direct ancestor.

# linear mound

mound built in the shape of a cigar or candy bar.

# line-guard

a device to fasten the retrieving line to a harpoon point.

## ■ line-level

a small spirit-bubble designed for suspension on a string. Used in archaeology to determine horizontal lines over short distances.

## ■ linguistic anthropology

a subdivision of anthropology that is concerned primarily with unwritten languages (both prehistoric and modern), with variation within languages and with the social uses of language. Traditionally divided into three branches: descriptive linguistics, the systematic study of the way language is constructed and used; historical linguistics, the study of the origin of language in general and of the evolution of the languages people speak today; and socio-linguistics, the study of the relationship between language and social relations.

## ■ linguistics

the scientific study of language.

## ■ lintel

wooden beam or stone slab lying horizontally above a doorway or window.

## ■ lipids

the class of compounds that includes fats, oils and waxes.

## ■ lithic industry

that part of an archaeological artefact assemblage that is manufactured of stone.

## ■ lithic technology

the process of manufacturing tools, etc., from stone. Most frequently refers to stone flaking.

## ■ lithic

1. of or pertaining to, stone.
2. stone tools or projectiles.

## ■ lithologic unit

litho-stratigraphic unit. A body of rock that is consistently dominated by a certain lithology or similar colour, mineralogic composition and grain size. It may be igneous, sedimentary or metamorphic and may or may not be consolidated.

■ **lithology**

the identification and study of rocks.

■ **littering**

unwanted debris.

■ **living**

having life, existing, in action or use.

■ **living floor**

the horizontal layer of an archaeological site that was once the surface occupied by a prehistoric group. It is identified both by the fact that it is hard-packed and also by the artefacts located on its surface.

■ **loan**

delivery of personal or institutional property by one person or institution to another in trust for a specific pur-

pose. This is done with th understanding that when th purpose is accomplished, th property is returned to th owner.

■ **lobate**

a type of stem that describe points and knives wit curved or rounded ears.

■ **lobbed**

a term used to describe th base portion of a point o blade that is eared. The ear are rounded and are forme by the meeting of two circle creating a lobbed effect. A object with an oval shape base or stem.

■ **locality**

a very large site or site-are composed of 2 or more con centrations or clusters of cul tural remains.

■ **loess sediments**

deposits formed of a yellowish dust of silt-sised particles blown by the wind and re-deposited on land newly de-glaciated or on sheltered areas.

■ **logistics**

the process of transporting, supplying and supporting a field project.

■ **long-house**

the long multi-family dwellings of the Iroquois area.

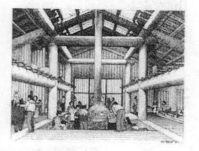

■ **looter**

one who steals from archaeological sites for personal gain.

■ **lossy compression**

any process for compressing an image file that causes the file, once uncompressed, to differ from the original appearance of the image file. Many lossy compression file formats look very similar to the uncompressed file, as the information that is discarded is often not easy to identify visually.

■ **lot**

a group of artefacts identified by provenience, material and/or object name. Provenience should be as specific as is recorded by the archaeologist. Material may not be mixed, such as glass and ceramics. Object name may be used to separate out different types of objects of the same material from the same provenience, e.g., flakes, projectile points.

■ **lux**

Lumens per square metre. Lux is a measure for visible light.

■ **maastrichtian**

European stage of the Upper Cretaceous, spanning the time between 72 and 66 million years ago.

■ **machine-readable records**

archives and records with informational content that is usually in code and is most efficiently read with the aid of a machine. Coded information is retrievable only by a machine. If not coded, the information may be read without the assistance of a machine. For example, micro-format is a machine-readable record, yet may be read without a machine.

# macro-blade

a large blade, greater than 5 cm in length.

# macro-family

classificatory term in linguistics, referring to a group of language families showing sufficient similarities to suggest that they are genetically related, e.g. the Nostratic macro-family is seen by some linguists as a unit embracing the Indo-European, Afro-Asiatic, Uralic, Altaic and Kartvelian language families.

# macrofossil

a fossil that is large enough to be studied without a microscope.

# magnetometer

instrument that detect changes in the earth's mag netic field. Used by archae ologists to detect and ma historic features and artefact both in the ground and un derwater.

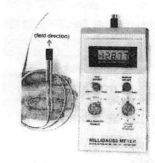

# manichean

a believer in religious or philosophical dualism, from a religious dualism originating in Persia in the third century A.D. and teaching the release of the spirit from matter through strict self-denial.

# man-made changes

any change caused by humans.

# mano

a stone with a flat side that was primarily used to grind

edible substances, typically corn, grains and nut meats.

## mano and metate

stone implements used for grinding nuts, seeds and other foodstuffs.

## mano

a hand-held stone used for grinding vegetable foods on a stone slab or 'metate'.

## mansio

an inn, especially for government officials.

## manuport

an unmodified, natural rock, brought into a site by human agency, that shows no sign of alteration.

## map key

used to show features on a map.

## map scale

used to show distance on a map.

## map-measure

a small wheeled device for measuring map distances.

## mapping

drawing a map showing the physical features of a community, usually an early step in a field project.

## market exchange

a mode of exchange which implies both a specific location for transactions and the sort of social relations where bargaining can occur. It usually involves a system of price making through negotiation.

■ **Marxist anthropology**

based principally on the writings of Karl Marx and Friedrich Engels, this posits a materialist model of societal change. Change within a society is seen as the result of contradictions arising between the forces of production (technology) and the relations of production (social organi-sation). Such contradictions are seen to emerge as a struggle between distinct social classes. Current Marxist anthropology focuses on the transformation of social orders and the relationships between conflict and cultural change.

■ **mastaba**

ancient Egyptian tomb used before the construction of the pyramids.

■ **material culture**

the buildings, tools and oth artefacts that includes ar material item that has ha cultural meaning ascribed it, in the past and present.

■ **material remains**

artefacts, objects, specimer and other physical evidenc that are excavated or re moved in connection wit efforts to locate, evaluate document, study, preserv or recover a prehistoric c historic resource.

■ **matrix**

the material that archaeolog cal artefacts are surrounded b before being excavated.

■ **maul**

a stone pounding tool that wa pecked, ground, grooved and hafted.

■ **Maya calendar**

a method employed by the Maya, of measuring the passage of time, comprising two separate calendar systems:
1. the Calendar Round, used for everyday purposes.
2. the Long Count, used for the reckoning of historical dates.

■ **Median ridge**

a ridge that usually runs from the tip of a blade to the hafting area which was formed by collateral flaking techniques in the manufacture of the artefact. The median ridge can be the thickest part of the blade.

■ **medicinal**

items use for a medical purpose, usually to cure or relieve a disease.

■ **mega fauna**

1. name given to the large ice age animals, i.e. mammoths and mastodons, that inhabited North America at the time of arrival of the Early Americans.

2. all animals weighing more than 100 pounds.

■ **megalithic yard**

a metrological unit (c. 2.72 ft.) proposed by Alexander Thom and argued by him, on statistical grounds, as the standard unit of length used in the construction of megalithic monuments in Britain and France.

■ **Memorandum Of Agreement (MOA)**

document prepared under Section 106 of the National Historic Preservation Act. A MOA details an agreement between parties such as the Advisory Council on Historic Preservation and a federal agency, on what may be done to resolve any adverse effects of an action on the cultural environment.

■ **mesolithic**

an Old World chronological period beginning around 10,000 years ago, situated between the Palaeolithic and the Neolithic and associated with the rise to dominance of microliths.

## mesozoic

an era of geologic time between the Palaeozoic and the Cenozoic, spanning the time between 248 and 65 million years ago. The word Mesozoic is from Greek and means 'middle life'.

## metadata

refers to documentation about data, such as descriptions of electronic files that effectively tell you the format, structure, contents and authority of the materials. Metadata standards, such as the Dublin Core and the Encoded Archival Description Standards, are developed and being adopted or adapted.

## metal detector

an electronic instrument which detects buried metallic objects by inducing and measuring an electromagnetic field.

## metallographic examination

a technique used in the study of early metallurgy involving the microscopic examination of a polished section cut from an artefact, which has been etched so as to reveal the metal structure.

## methodological individualism (or individualistic method)

approach to the study of societies which assumes that thoughts and decisions do have agency and that actions and shared institutions can be interpreted as the products of the decisions and actions of individuals.

## microblade core

the nucleus from which micro-blades were manufactured. Usually, a small barrel or conical shaped stone artefact with a flat top and one or more fluted surfaces left as scars from the removal of the microblades.

■ **microblade**

a small prismatic parallel-sided flake struck from a prepared core. Microblades were probably inserted end-to-end in a slotted bone or antler shaft to provide a continuous cutting edge for points or knives.

■ **microfaunal remains**

very small animal remains, such as rodent bones, tiny bone fragments, insects, small molluscs, foraminifera, etc., discovered in an archaeological site.

■ **microfloral remains**

very small plant materials such as seeds, pollen, spores, phytoliths, etc., discovered in an archaeological site. Microfauna and microflora are extremely important in palaeo-environmental reconstruction.

■ **microform**

microforms are photographic images that are 20 to 150 times smaller than the original. It is generally pro-duced on film that has a life expectancy of 500 years, commonly called microfilm.

■ **microfossil**

a fossil so small that it must be studied with a microscope.

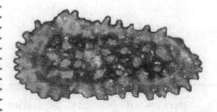

■ **microlith**

a tiny stone tool, characteristic of the Mesolithic period, many of which were probably used as barbs.

■ **micrometer**

a unit of measure, there are one million micrometers in one meter.

■ **microwear analysis**

the study of the patterns of wear or damage on the edge of stone tools, which provides valuable information on the way in which the tool was used.

■ **midden**

the band or layer of soil which contains the by products of human activity as a result of the accumulation of these materials on their living surface. For prehistoric sites, a layer of soil that was stained to a dark colour by the decomposition of organic waste, which also contains food bones, fragments of stone tools, charcoal, pieces of pottery or other discarded materials. For historic sites, a similar layer of soil but with appropriate historic material remains often in a much thinner deposit. These deposits can be seen as strata and oftentimes when more than one strata of midden is present in a site and are clearly defined, each strata can be called a lens.

■ **middle archaic**

a cultural period of the north American aborigine Indians, dating from 7,000 to 4,000 b.p.

■ **middle range theory**

a conceptual framework linking raw archaeological data with higher-level generalisations and conclusions about the past which can be derived from this evidence.

■ **midline**

an imaginary line extending along the centre of a projectile, from the distal tip to the midpoint of the basal edge.

■ **midpoint**

an imaginary point at the intersection of the midline and the transverse line.

■ **midwestern taxonomic system**

a framework devised by McKern (1939) to systematise sequences in the Great Plains area of the United States, using the general principle of similarities between artefact assemblages.

■ **miocene**

a epoch of the upper Tertiary period, spanning the time between 23.8 and 5.3 million years ago. It is named after the Greek words 'meion' (less) and 'ceno' (new).

■ **mission statement**

also called a 'statement of purpose', a document drawn up by a repository to succinctly outline its purpose, current scope and uses of its collections and immediate goals.

■ **Mississippi River**

river to the east of Iowa.

■ **mississippian**

a cultural period of the South Eastern north American aborigine Indians, dating from 1,300 to 400 b.p. , this culture shows strong Mexican influences and is associated with many groups ancestral to the historic muskhogean speaking tribes of the southeast. Note that this cultural period does not relate to North Eastern central or western north American aborigine Indians.

■ **Minimum Number Of Individuals (MNI)**

a method of assessing species abundance in faunal assemblages based on a calculation of the smallest number of animals necessary to account for all the identified bones. Usually calculated from the most abundant bone or tooth from either the left or right side of the animal.

■ **mobiliary art**

a term used for the portable art of the Ice Age, comprising engravings and carvings on small objects of stone, antler, bone and ivory.

■ **mocronate tip**

a type of distal end or tip treatment in which a small sharp nipple has been left on the very tip of the blade.

■ **model**

a system of hypothetical principles that represents the characters of a phenomenon and from which predictions can be made.

■ **mould**

a cavity left in firm sediment by the decayed body of an organism.

■ **monocausal explanation**

the attribution of one cause to the existence of a phenomenon.

■ **monogram**

set of letters combined into one (used of Chi-Rho).

■ **moraine**

a glacial deposit (till) with a distinctive topographic expression. 'Terminal moraines' mark episodes of stability or re-advance in a Period of overall glacial retreat. Moraines appear as hill or ridges marking original glacial limits.

■ **morphology**

1. the overall projectile form outline of the artefact. Typically, falling into one of the following 8 major classifications; *lanceolate, auriculate, basal notched, stemmed, corner notched, side notched, stemmed-bifurcated.*

2. the study of form and structure of animals and plants, and their fossil remains.

■ **mortises and tenons**

a method of carpentry joinery where holes are chiselled as receptacles (mortises) for chiseled projections (tenons) on wooden beams.

■ **mosaic**

floor composed of pieces of coloured tesserae to form geometric or figured designs.

# mosaic evolution

the concept that major evolutionary changes tend to take place in stages, not all at once. Human evolution shows a mosaic pattern in the fact that small canine teeth, large brains and tool use did not all evolve at the same time.

# mossbauer spectroscopy

a technique used in the analysis of artefact composition, particularly iron compounds in pottery. It involves the measurement of the gamma radiation absorbed by the iron nuclei, which provides information on the particular iron compounds in the sample. and hence on the conditions of firing when the pottery was being made.

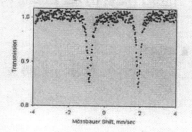

# mottled

any material that contains spots of different colours or shades.

# multicausal explanation

the attribution of more than one cause to the existence of a phenomenon.

# multi-component

a site is said to be multi-component when it shows evidence of 2 or more distinctive cultural occupations.

# Multi-Dimensional Scaling (MDSCAL)

a multivariate statistical technique which aims to develop spatial structure from numerical data by estimating the differences and similarities between analytical units.

# ■ multilineal evolutionism

an anthropological approach that focuses on the development of individual cultures or populations without insfisting that all follow the same evolutionary pattern.

# ■ multiplier effect

a term used in systems thinking to describe the process by which changes in one field of human activity (subsystem) sometimes act to promote changes in other fields (subsystems) and in turn act on the original subsystem itself. An instance of positive feedback, it is thought by some to be one of the primary mechanisms of societal change.

# ■ multivariate explanation

explanation of culture change, e.g. the origin of the state, which, in contrast to monocausal approaches, stresses the interaction of several factors operating simultaneously.

# ■ mummy

a preserved body wrapped in cloth. Ancient Egyptian mummified their dead, believing it was necessary for them to enter the after-life.

# ■ museum

a permanent, non-profit organisation, essentially educational and often aesthetic in purpose, which, utilising professional staff, acquires tangible objects, interprets them, cares for them and exhibits them to the public on a regular basis.

# ■ myth

a tradition, fable or an invented story.

# ■ National Historic Landmarks Program

authorised under the Historic Sites Act of 1935, it coordinates, manages and preserves historic and archaeological sites that have been designated by the Secretary of the Interior to have national significance and illustrate the nation's heritage.

# ■ National Historic Preservation Act of 1966

public law 89-665, as amended by public law 96515, National Historic Preservation Act Amendments of 1980, 94 stat. 2987. This act and its amendments clearly established the basic funding and implementation of archaeological work in federally funded projects.

# ■ National Park Proclamation

special distinction given to an area for the preservation and public education of a historic site.

# ■ National Park Service

established within the U.S. Department of the Interior in 1916, to manage the National Park System, which today comprises approximately 380 national parks, national historic sites, national battlefields, national seashores and other 'national' designations. The National Park Service is the chief agency in the federal government charged with protecting archaeological and historic sites of national significance.

# ■ National Register Of Historic Places (NRHP)

1.the administrative branch of the department of interior that officially reviews nominations of archaeological and historic sites and structures and guides the federal implementation of cultural resources legislation.

2.list of districts, sites, buildings, structures and objects determined to be of historic, cultural, archi-tectural, archaeological or engineering significance at the national, state or local level. The name also applies to the NPS staff unit that processes and manages the list and manages the extensive archives of property records in the Register.

■ **Native American**
of or relating to, a tribe, people or culture that is indigenous to the United States. Synonymous to 'American Indian'.

■ **native copper**
metallic copper found naturally in nuggets, which can be worked by hammering, cutting and annealing.

■ **natural changes**
any change as a result of weather or other normal occurrence.

■ **natural levels (also 'stratigraphic levels')**
an excavation level defined by the original stratigraphic units of the site.

■ **natural resource**
a material that comes from the earth.

■ **natural selection**
the process whereby members of a species, who have more surviving offspring than others, pass their traits on to the next generation, whereas the less favoured do not do so to the same degree.

■ **nature**
environment.

■ **neck**
that part of the projectile or blade that is narrowest and is in between the notches. Represents the topmost part

of the hafting area of a notched artefact.

# negative
an effect that is not in the best interest of something.

# negative feedback
in systems thinking, this is a process which acts to counter or 'dampen' the potentially disruptive effects of external inputs. It acts as a stabilising mechanism.

# nektonic
used to describe aquatic organisms that swim.

# neolithic revolution
a term coined by V.G. Childe in 1941, to describe the origin and consequences of farming, i.e. the development of stock raising and agriculture, allowing the widespread development of settled village life.

# neolithic
an Old World chronological period characterised by the development of agriculture

and, hence, an increasing emphasis on sedentism.

# nephrite
a hard fibrous green to white rock often used for the manufacture of adze-blades. Commonly called jade.

# net sinker (also 'net weight', 'sinker')
a rock used to submerge a fishing net, may be grooved, notched or perforated.

# Neutron Activation Analysis (NAA)
a method used in the analysis of artefact composition which depends on the excitation of the nuclei of the atoms of a sample's various elements, when these are bombarded with slow neutrons. The method is accu-

rate to about plus or minus 5 percent.

## neutron scattering

a remote sensing technique involving the placing of a probe into the soil, in order to measure the relative rates of neutron flows through the soil. Since stone produces a lower count rate than soil, buried features can often be detected.

## new archaeology

a new approach advocated in the 1960s which argued for an explicitly scientific framework of archaeological method and theory, with hypothesis rigorously tested, as the proper basis for explanation rather than simply description.

## Number Of Identified Specimens (NISP)

a gross counting technique used in the quantification of animal bones. The method may produce misleading results in assessing the relative abundance of different species, since skeletal differences and differential rates of bone preservation mean that some species will be represented more than others.

## nodule

a large, usually roughly spherical piece of stone such as flint which was selected as a material from which to remove flakes or blades for the manufacture of stone tools and projectile points.

## non-cultural artefacts or materials

general term applied to items collected at archaeological sites that are natural not man-made, but still have cultural or archaeological significance. Includes soil samples, shell and floral remains.

## non-equilibrium systems

see self-organisation.

## non-living
matter or material that is not alive.

## non-probabilistic sampling
a non-statistical sampling strategy (in contrast to probabilistic sampling) which concentrates on sampling areas on the basis of intuition, historical documentation or long field experience in the area.

## non-renewable resource
something that can not be replaced.

## notch
a flaked u or v shaped indentation.

## notch width
the measurement of the space between the notches

across the narrowest point of the stem or base.

## notch, basal
a flaking technique applied to accommodate hafting which involved the flaking of notches into the basal edge of a preform.

## notched, corner
a flaking technique applied to accommodate hafting which involved the flaking of notches into the corners of a preform.

## notched, low side
a flaking technique applied to accommodate hafting which involved the flaking of notches into the side of a preform near its base.

## notched, side
a major projectile form where notches to accommodate hafting were struck into the sides of a preform near the base.

## notches, expanded
notches which are broader near the stem than between

the auricle and barb tips. These notches are bigger at their end than at the blade edge.

■ **notochord**

a rodlike cord of cells in lower chordates that forms the main lengthwise support structure of the body.

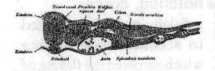

■ **nucleation**

the tendency of populations to cluster in settlements of increasing size and density.

■ **observer**

one who observes; a spectator who takes notice of something.

■ **obsidian**

a type of black stone (volcanic glass) that may be clear, black, brown or green in colour, whose ease of working and characteristically hard flint like edges allow it to be used for the making of tools which is one of the finest raw materials for the chipping of stone tools, found in the Western U.S.

■ **obsidian hydration dating**

this technique involves the absorption of water on exposed surfaces of obsidian. When the local hydration rate is known, the thickness of the hydration layer, if accurately measured, can be used to provide an absolute date.

■ **obtuse**

a term used to describe a rounded tip or blunt tipped artefact.

■ **ochre**

iron oxide or hematite. Colour is commonly reddish-brown to yellow. Used as a natural pigment.

## ■ off-site data

evidence from a range of information, including scatters of artefacts and features such as plough marks and field boundaries, that provides important evidence about human exploitation of the environment.

## ■ oldowan industry

the earliest toolkits, comprising flake and pebble tools, used by hominids in the Olduvai Gorge, East Africa.

## ■ oligocene

an epoch of the early Tertiary period, spanning the time between 33.7 and 23.8 million years ago. It is named after the Greek words 'oligos' (little, few) and 'ceno' (new).

## ■ open pit mine

a large scale mining operation that removes materials from the surface of a site. A large hole or 'pit' remains unless the land is reshaped.

## ■ open-area excavation

the opening up of large horizontal areas for excavation, used especially where single period deposits lie close to the surface as, for example, with the remains of American Indian or European Neolithic long houses.

## ■ Optical Emission Spectrometry (OES)

a technique used in the analysis of artefact composition, based on the principle that electrons, when excited, i.e. heated to a high temperature, release light of a particular wavelength. The presence or absence of various elements is established by examining the appropriate spectral line of their characteristic wavelengths. Generally, this method gives an accuracy of only 25 percent and has been superseded by ICPS (Inductively Coupled Plasma Emission Spectrometry).

■ **oral history**

verbally transmitted information about past events. Although often providing information about non-written events, such history is subject to the vagaries of human perceptions and mental recall.

■ **ordovician**

the second earliest period of the Palaeozoic era, spanning the time between 505 and 440 million years ago. It is named after a Celtic tribe called the Ordovices.

■ **original order**

the functional filing arrangement imposed on a document collection by its creator. The original order of collections can provide information not found elsewhere, such as 'when' the creator received a communication, 'who' reviewed a document or 'what' the sequence of an administrative activity was. Original order should be preserved or reconstructed in a collection, as it allows for rapid arrangement, accurate contextual research and additional insight into the record creator's methods and activities. If a collection has no order because of mismanagement or disaster, a decision to impose an order may be made only by an experienced archivist.

■ **osteodontokeratic culture**

an archaeological culture based upon tools made of bone, teeth and hoary.

■ **osteology**

the study of bones.

■ **ostracoderms**

primitive jawless fishes, covered by bony armour, that lived in the Cambrian through Devonian periods.

■ **ostracum**

fragments (as of pottery) containing inscriptions. The singular is 'ostraca'.

■ **outbuildings**

a term used to refer to all non-residential structures on a site. These include animal pens, storage buildings, sheds, barns, etc.

■ **outcrops**

a term designating the surface exposure of rock layers, which have not been decomposed into soil.

■ **outline**

a key and obvious diagnostic feature is the outline or silhouette of the implement. The outline is the two dimensional image perceived when viewing the outer perimeter of an artefact with a blade face towards the viewer. Some projectile point types have distinctive outlines and can be accurately identified by this singular feature.

■ **outwash channel**

a stream valley formed by glacial melt-water.

■ **outwash deposit**

fluvial sediments laid down by glacial melt-water.

■ **palaestra**

exercise yard of a public bath-house, in Britain sometimes covered.

■ **paleo**

a cultural period of the north American aborigine Indians, defined as 40,000 to 12,000 b.p.

■ **paleoanthropology**

the study of the fossil record and archaeology.

■ **paleobathymetry**

the study of ocean depths and topography of the ocean floor in the geologic past.

■ **paleobiogeography**

the branch of palaeontology that deals with the geographic distribution of plants and animals in past geologic time, especially with regard to ecology, climate and evolution.

■ **paleoceanography**
the study of oceans in the geologic past, including its physical, chemical, biologic and geologic aspects.

■ **paleocene**
earliest epoch of the Tertiary period, spanning the time between 65 and 55.5 million years ago. It is named after the Greek words 'palaois' (old) and 'ceno' (new).

■ **paleoclimate**
the climate of a given period of time in the geologic past.

■ **paleodemography**
study of ancient human populations.

■ **paleoecology**
the study of the relationship of ancient organisms or groups of organisms to their environments.

■ **paleoentomology**
the study of insects from archaeological contexts. The survival of insect exoskel-etons, which are quite resistant to decomposition, is an important source of evidence in the reconstruction of palaeo-environments.

■ **paleoenvironments**
past environmental/climatic conditions.

■ **paleoethnobotany (archaeobotany)**
the recovery and identification of plant remains from archaeological contexts, important in the reconstruction of past environments and economies.

■ **paleoindian**
a term most frequently applied to early projectile point 'cultures' of North America (e.g. Clovis, Folsom, Cody, etc.).

■ **paleolithic**
1. a stage of the history of mankind which is characterised by the use and manufacture of stone tools (lithics).
2. the archaeological period before c.10,000 BC, charac-

terised by the earliest known stone tool manufacture.

■ **paleomagnetism**
see **archaeomagnetic dating**.

■ **paleontologists**
experts on animal life of the distant past, one who studies fossils.

■ **paleontology**
that specialised branch of physical anthropology that analyses the emergence and subsequent evolution of human physiology.

■ **paleopathology**
the study of the evidence of trauma and disease in fossilised skeletons.

■ **paleosol**
'old soil', buried soil horizons indicative of past soil conditions different from that presently prevailing.

■ **paleozoic**
an era of geologic time, from the end of the Precambrian to the beginning of the Mesozoic, spanning the time be-

tween 544 and 248 million years ago. The word Palaeozoic is from Greek and means 'old life'.

■ **palisade (also 'stockade')**
a fence formed of vertical posts placed side-by-side. Usually intended for defensive purposes.

■ **palynologist**
one who studies plant pollen and spores. Since pollen may be preserved thousands of years, it can be used to reconstruct the plant ecology of the past.

■ **palynology**

the analysis of fossil pollen as an aid to the reconstruction of past vegetation and climates.

■ **paradigmatic view**

approach to science, developed by Thomas Kuhn, which holds that science develops from a set of assumptions (paradigm) and that revolutionary science ends with the acceptance of a new paradigm which ushers in a period of normal science.

■ **parallel flaking**

a technique used in the production of stone tools that is often found on the earliest projectile points from north central Texas. Long, consistent chipping scars run parallel on the flat sides of stone tools.

■ **parapet**

top of a Roman fortification, consisting of a wallwalk and battlements.

■ **parietal art**

a term used to designate art on the walls of caves and shelters or on huge blocks.

■ **patina**

a surface discolouration or adhesive outer crust of an artefact due to chemical changes resulting from weathering. Patina does not necessarily imply great age.

■ **patination**

a loss of minerals from the surface of an artefact which resulted in a colour change usually to a lighter side.

■ **pebble tool**

a natural rounded pebble manufactured into a simple cutting tool by the removal of a few percussion flakes, usually unifacially on one edge.

■ **pecking (also 'pecking and grinding')**

the process of manufacturing heavy-duty stone tools, like bowls, mauls, etc., from granular rocks by prolonged hammering with a hammerstone to form an intended shape by removal of very small chips. Abrasive techniques might be used to finish the piece.

■ **pedestal**
a raised area isolated around important excavated materials to facilitate their study.

■ **pediment**
triangular gabled end of a roof (usually used of temples).

■ **pedology**
the science that deals with the study of soils.

■ **peer-polity interaction**
the full range of exchanges taking place — including imitation, emulation, competition, warfare and the exchange of material goods and information — between autonomous (self-governing) socio-political units, generally within the same geographic region.

■ **pelagic**
referring to open water marine habitats, free of direct influence of the shore or ocean bottom. Pelagic organisms are generally free-swimming (nektonic) or floating (planktonic).

■ **pendant**
any ornamental object designed for suspension.

■ **pennsylvanian**
a period of the Palaeozoic era, spanning the time between 325 and 286 million years ago. It is named after the state of Pennsylvania, where rocks of this age are widespread.

■ **percussion flaking (also 'direct percussion flaking')**
the technique of shaping stone artefacts by removing flakes with direct blows, with a hammer of stone, antler or wood.

■ **periglacial phenomena (also 'cryoturbation')**
a general term for disturbance of surficial deposits caused by frost action. Most prevalent in areas of permafrost and can be very damaging to archaeological sites.

■ **period**
a unit of geological time, a division of an era.

■ **permian**
the final period of the Palaeozoic era, spanning the time between 286 and 248 million years ago. It is named after the province of Perm, Russia, where rocks of this age were first studied.

■ **pest management**
see **Integrated Pest Management**.

■ **petrified wood**
agatised wood, sometimes used as a raw material for the manufacture of flaked stone artefacts. Often banded or laminated and of variable colour.

■ **petroglyphs**
pictures, symbols or other art work pecked, carved or incised on natural rock surfaces which express artistic or religious meaning.

■ **petrology**
the study of rocks- a direct division of geology.

■ **pH level /pH scale**
a logarithmic measure of the acidity or alkalinity of material. The pH scale goes from 0 to 14, with each number indicating a ten-fold increase or decrease from the next number. A pH of 7 is neutral, less than 7 is acid, greater than 7 is basic or alkaline.

■ **phalanges**
human finger bones.

■ **phanerozoic**
the period of time, also known as an eon, between the end of the Precambrian and today, the Phanerozoic be-

gins with the start of the Cambrian period, 544 million years ago. It encompasses the period of abundant, complex life on the Earth.

# pharaoh
ancient Egyptian king.

# phase
1. a subdivision of a culture which can be defined as a reoccurring complex of archaeological traits that can be distinguished from any other similar complex. A phase usually involved a more limited territory and a briefer time span than a culture. Synonymous to a focus.
2. a chronologically limited cultural unit within a local culture sequence, characterised by sufficient diagnostic traits to set it apart from all other units. A phase is generally represented by 2 or more components in several sites and is the basic classificatory unit of archaeological 'cultures'.

# Phase I,II,III
terms primarily used in contract archaeology or cultural resources management, to note the type of archaeological fieldwork being carried out. Phase I typically refers to site reconnaissance survey and mapping to find and inventory sites. Phase II refers to intensive survey, collection and site testing. Phase III refers to full excavation or 'mitigation' for data recovery. Collections are made in each phase, although Phase III usually yields the largest and most complete collections based on the collecting strategy.

# photogrammetry
the science of obtaining accurate measurements and maps from photographs.

# photo-mosaic
a number of overlapping photographs glued together to provide continuous coverage of a large area. Aerial photographic mosaics are

used in the production of modern topographic maps.

■ **phyllite**

a soft laminated shale-like rock used for the manufacture of decorative objects such as pendants and beads.

■ **physical anthropology**

the scientific study of the physical characteristics, variability and evolution of the human organism.

■ **physical environment**

the complex of inanimate elements that surround an organism.

■ **phytoliths**

minute particles of silica derived from the cells of plants, able to survive after the organism has decomposed or has been burnt. They are common in ash layers, pottery and even on stone tools.

■ **pictographs**

aboriginally painted designs on natural rock surfaces. Red ochre is the most frequently used pigment, natural or abstract motifs may be represented which express artistic or religious meaning.

■ **piece esquillee (fr. 'splintered piece')**

a type of flaked stone artefact manufactured by the bipolar percussion technique. Generally characterised by a lenticular or wedge-shaped cross-section, opposed bifacial crushing, battering and hinge-fracturing, and frequently relatively long columnar 'blade-like' flake scars.

■ **pilae**

pillars of brick (or stone) supporting the floor of a room with a hypocaust.

■ **pilaster**

column or pillar incorporated in, but projecting from, a wall.

# ■ pinger (or boomer profiler)

an underwater survey device, more powerful than sidescan sonar, capable of probing up to 60 m (197 ft) below the seabed.

# ■ pipestone

a soft red sandstone, from a quarry in South western Minnesota, used in the manufacture of aboriginal smoking pipes.

# ■ piscina

swimming-bath in a public bath- house.

# ■ piston corer

a device for extracting columns of sediment from the ocean floor. Dates for the different layers are obtained by radiocarbon, archaeo-

magnetic or uranium series methods.

# ■ pithouse

A semi-subterranean 'earth-lodge' dwelling. Usually consisted of an earth-covered log framework roof over a circular to rectangular excavation.

# ■ placoderms

A peculiar group of primitive armoured jawed fish, found almost exclusively in rocks from the Devonian Period.

# ■ plane-table mapping

the construction of small-scale topographic maps, on the site, by use of an alidade, plane-table and stadia-rod.

# ■ plane-table

a small drawing table mounted on a tripod in such a way that it can be levelled and rotated. Provides the base for the alidade in plane-table mapping.

■ **plankton**

aquatic organisms that drift or swim weakly.

■ **planktonic**

used to describe aquatic organisms that float.

■ **plano convex**

a description of a cross-section of a blade that is semi-circular. One face is flat while the other face is excurvate or rounded. Also sometimes referred to as a uniface cross-section.

■ **plating**

a method of bonding metals together, for instance silver with copper or copper with gold.

■ **pleistocene epoch**

a period of time dated from 1.6 million to 11,500 years ago. It was characterised by an unstable climate with arctic conditions in the form of glaciers which spread down from the poles at least four times.

■ **pleistocene**

a geologic period, sometimes referred to as the 'Ice Age', which began about 1.6 million years ago and ended with the melting of the large continental glaciers creating the modern climatic pattern about 11,500 years ago. Some North American archaeologists specialise in the investigation of sites containing the remains of extinct animals such as the woolly mammoth that were hunted by Palaeo-Indian groups between about 12,000 and 8,000 years ago at the end of the Pleistocene.

■ **plinth**

projecting course at the foot of a wall, also used of a base, e.g. for an altar.

■ **pliocene**

final epoch of the Tertiary period, spanning the time between 5.3 and 1.8 million years ago. It is named after the Greek words 'pleion' (more) and 'ceno' (new).

# plummet

a problematic polished stone artefact that has many conjectured intended uses. In all likelihood, a ceremonial object.

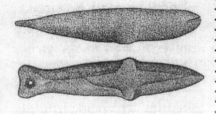

# podium

raised platform (especially used of temples).

# political economy approach

assumes that peasants rationally calculate the advantages.

# polity

a politically independent or autonomous social unit, whether simple or complex, which may in the case of a complex society (such as a state) comprise many lesser dependent components.

# pollen analysis

see **palynology.**

# pollution

contamination of soil, water or air.

# polyethylene

a chemically stable, flexible, transparent or translucent plastic. May be found in the form of film, sheets, foam and rods. It is widely used for making archival quality plastic bags and sleeves.

# polymer

a chemical compound or mixture of compounds (like or unlike) formed of repeating structural units. All plastics are polymers.

# polypropylene

similar to polyethylene only stiffer and more heat resistant. Commonly used to make sleeves for slides or film or small containers.

# polyurethane

an unstable polymer that should not be used for storage or in repositories. Tends to off-gas, which can create chemical reactions on or in objects.

■ **polyvinyl acetate (pa) emulsion**
a colourless, transparent polymer of vinyl acetate upon drying, that is used in adhesives.

■ **polyvinyl chloride (pvc)**
a plastic polymer. Not as chemically stable as other plastics because it may emit hydrochloric acid as it deteriorates. Its use for preservation is limited for that reason.

■ **portal**
doorway or carriageway, especially of a fort-gateway.

■ **positive**
an effect that is certain to be good for something.

■ **positive feedback**
a term used in systems thinking to describe a response in which changing output conditions in the system stimu-

late further growth in the input. It is one of the principal factors in generating system change or morphogenesis.

■ **positivism**
theoretical position that explanations must be empirically verifiable, that there are universal laws in the structure and transformation of human institutions and that theories which incorporate individualistic elements, such as minds, are not verifiable.

■ **post-contact period (also 'historic period')**
refers to the period following the first arrival of Europeans.

■ **postern**
minor gate or door in a late Roman town- or fortwall.

■ **post-hole**
hole dug to receive a wooden upright.

■ **posting-station**
small town on a main road, where travelling officials could find an inn (mansio).

# ■ post-mold

the impression, stain or cavity, left in the ground by a rotted wooden post.

# ■ postprocessual explanation

explanation formulated in reaction to the perceived limitations of functional-processual archaeology. It eschews generalisation in favour of an 'individualising' approach that is influenced by structuralism, Critical theory and neo-Marxist thought.

# ■ pot hunter

1. person who digs or picks up archaeological materials without permission in order to recover goods.
2. an 'amateur archaeologist' who vandalises and destroys sites to add to his private collection or for monetary gain.

# ■ pot sherd (shard)

an individual piece of a broken pottery vessel.

# ■ potassium argon dating

a chronometric dating technique based on the rate of decay of potassium 40 to argon 40. Used to date rocks up to thousands of millions of years old, though it is restricted to volcanic material no more recent than c 100 000 years old. One of the most widely used methods in the dating of early hominid sites in Africa.

# ■ pot-lid fracture

a circular flake removed from crypto-crystalline materials by sudden heating. Leaves a small saucer-shaped depression in the surface of the stone.

# ■ preadaptation

the potential to adapt to a new niche.

# ■ precambrian

all geologic time before the beginning of the Palaeozoic era. This includes about 90% of all geologic time and spans the time from the beginning of the earth, about

4.5 billion years ago, to 544 million years ago. Its name means 'before Cambrian.'

■ **pre-ceramic period**
the period prior to the introduction of ceramic artefacts.

■ **pre-contact**
refers to the period before the first arrival of Europeans in a given area.

■ **preform**
an early preliminary stage in the reduction-manufacture of a flaked stone artefact. Preforms which ar roughly shaped were intended to be finished at a later date into a point or blade. In general, preform was a finished 'blank' that locked only the knapping of the hafting area details for completion of the final implement.

■ **prehistoric hunter**
gatherers-humans who lived prior to written history and depended upon the hunting of wild animals and the gathering of natural plant foods for their livelihood.

■ **prehistoric sites**
locations where people, who were alive before modern written records existed, once lived, hunted, camped or were buried. Painted or carved rock outcrops are considered sites as well.

■ **prehistoric**
the period prior to written records for any given area.

■ **prehistory**
the period of human history before the advent of writing.

■ **preservation potential**
the probability of a bone's being preserved after death.

■ **pressure flaking**
the technique of shaping tools from crypto-crystalline or fine-grained rocks by pressing off small conchoidal flakes by flaking. Tools of antler or bone.

■ **prestige goods**
a term used to designate a limited range of exchange

goods to which a society ascribes high status or value.

### previous blade or flake scar

a blade or flake scar seen on the face of a blade or flake, resulting from the initial removal of a blade or a flake from a core or nodule.

### pre-wisconsinan

prior to the Wisconsinan glacial period or older than about 70,000 b.p.

### primary context

the original depositional situation, unaffected by any later disturbance.

### primary deposit

a primary deposit is a body of sediments which have not been significantly disturbed since their original deposition.

### primary flakes

the first series of flakes removed from a core or nucleus in the process of tool manufacture.

### primitive valuables

a term coined by Dalton to describe the tokens of wealth and prestige, often of specially valued items, that were used in the ceremonial exchange systems of non-state societies. Examples include the shell necklaces and bracelets of the kula systems.

### principia

headquarters building of a Roman fort.

### probabilistic sampling

sampling method, employing probability theory, designed to draw reliable general conclusions about a site or region, based on small sample areas. Four types of sampling strategies are recognised:

1. simple random sampling.

2. stratified random sampling.

3. systematic sampling.

4. stratified systematic sampling.

■ **processing, initial**

a series of steps undertaken on an archaeological collection prior to its deposit for long-term curation, often including cleaning, labelling, packing and cataloguing.

■ **processual archaeology**

an approach that stresses the dynamic relationship between social and economic aspects of culture and the environment as the basis for understanding the processes of culture change. Uses the scientific methodology of problem statement, hypothesis formulation and subsequent testing. The earlier functional-processual archaeology has been contrasted with cognitive-processual archaeology, where the emphasis is on integrating ideological and symbolic aspects.

■ **procurator**

government financial administrator.

■ **profile drawing**

a precise scale drawing of the strata and horizons revealed in the walls of an excavation or other exposure. A section of a site that has been drawn, is said to have been 'profiled'.

■ **profile**

a section or exposure of the ground showing depositional or developmental strata or horizons.

■ **project design**

see **research design**.

■ **projectile point**

1.the tip of an arrow or atlatl dart, often made out of stone, a sharp, penetrating distal tip, which is usually flaked stone that was used in conjunction with a spear, dart or arrow. Also can be made from ground and polished stone, antler, bone, shell or metal.

2. an inclusive term for arrow, spear or dart-points. Characterised by a symmetrical point, a relatively thin cross-section and some element to allow attachment to the projectile shaft. Flaked stone projectile points are usually classified by their outline form.

■ **proterozoic**

the final era of the Precambrian, spanning the time between 2.5 billion and 544 million years ago. Fossils of both primitive single celled and more advanced multicellular organisms begin to appear in abundance in rocks from this era. Its name means 'early life'.

■ **protist**

an organism that belongs to the kingdom Protista, which includes forms with both plant and animal affinities, i.e., protozoans, bacteria and some algae, fungi and viruses.

■ **protohistoric**

a period prior to the beginning of written records in an area, but after that area has been initially mentioned in reports written elsewhere.

■ **proton magnetometer**

a device used in subsurface detection which records variation in the earth's magnetic field.

■ **provenience**

pertaining to the origin or source of an artefact, typically the geographic location from where the artefact was found. The three-dimensional location of an artefact or feature within an archaeological site, measured by two horizontal dimensions and a vertical elevation.

■ **provisional site designation**

a temporary code or number applied to newly located sites during site-surveying, until a final Borden System number can be assigned.

■ **proximal corners**
the parts of a blade nearest the stem which define the outermost ends of the blade edge if the stem were ignored or removed. Also referred to as the barb.

■ **proximal portion**
the part of a blade nearest the stem of hafting area or in the area of a tool nearest the basal edge.

■ **proximal**
the portion of an artefact or bone closest to the body of the user or 'owner'.

■ **pseudo-archaeology**
the use of selective archaeological evidence to promulgate non-scientific, fictional accounts of the past.

■ **psoralea ssp**
the prairie turnip, as it is commonly referred to, is actually several species of plants which grow underground tubers. Only one species was actually recorded as having been used by plains Indians and only recently has any archaeological evidence for the use of this plant been recovered.

■ **public archaeology**
a movement to increase public awareness and education about archaeology, which advanced the legislative attempts to provide funding and protection for archaeological sites.

■ **public archaeology**
a branch of modern archaeology that focusses on increasing public awareness and education about archaeology and that promotes legislative attempts to provide funding and protection for archaeological sites.

■ **punctates**
impressions on the surface of ceramic vessels made by implements or by fingernails, as a form of decoration.

■ **punctuated equilibria**
principal feature of the evolutionary theory propounded by Niles Eldredge and Stephen J. Gould, in which species change is represented as a form of Darwinian gradualism 'punctuated' by periods of rapid evolutionary change.

■ **putlog holes**
row(s) of square or rectangular holes in a masonry wall which held horizontal scaffolding timbers during construction. On completion of the work they were plugged with loose material, since fallen out.

■ **pyramid**
structure built by the ancient Egyptians as tombs and the ancient Americans as temples.

■ **pyrotechnology**
the intentional use and control of fire by humans.

■ **quadrant**
generally refers to one-quarter of an excavation unit or level, e.g. 'the northwest quadrant of excavation unit N. 2-4, E. 4-6'.

■ **quadrat**
a rectangular sampling unit.

■ **quarry blank**
see **preform**.

■ **quarry site**
a site where lithic raw materials have been mined.

■ **quarry**
location where humans mine minerals from.

■ **quartz**
a material frequently used in projectile points and other artefacts. When quartz is clear and colourless, it is called rock crystal, milky quartz is milky white, smoky quartz is clouded a brown colour, rose quartz is a pale red colour, sugar quartz is the colour of brown sugar.

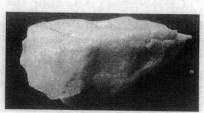

■ **quartz, sugar**

also known as quartzite, a granular low grade form of light brownish quartz used in the production of some point types, especially in areas where flint or cherts were not available.

■ **quartz-crystal**

pure silicate rock-crystal. Usually perfectly clear with six crystal surfaces. May be used as a raw material for lithic tool manufacture.

■ **quartzite**

a granular form of quartz stone, commonly white, yellow or red which was formed in water deposited sediments and consists of sand grains which have been cemented together. It can be chipped, but is difficult to work.

■ **quaternary**

the second period of the Cenozoic era, spanning the time between 1.8 million years ago and the present. It contains two epochs: the Pleistocene and the Ho-

locene. It is named after the Latin word 'quatern' (four at a time).

■ **radioactive decay**

the regular process by which radioactive isotopes break down into their decay products with a half-life which is specific to the isotope in question.

■ **radiocarbon dating**

a process that provides absolute dates by counting the radioactive decay of carbon in the remains of once living plants and animals, i.e., charcoal, wood, bone, shell. Using the known half-life of Carbon-14 and measuring the amount of un-decayed carbon-14 in animal or plant remains, an age bracket of the remains and an associated artefact or feature can be determined.

■ **radioimmunoassay**

a method of protein analysis, whereby it is possible to identify protein molecules surviving in fossils which are thousands and even millions of years old.

## ■ radiometric dating

a type of chronometric dating that involves methods based upon the decay of radioactive materials. Examples are radiocarbon and potassium-argon dating.

## ■ raised beaches

these are remnants of former coastlines, usually the result of processes such as isostatic uplift or tectonic movements.

## ■ random sample

a sample in which each individual in a population has the same chance of being selected as any other.

## ■ range of variation

in archaeology, it is the extent of differences that exists between items in an artefact class. For artefacts, variation can exist and be measured for variables such as time period, size, style, material and technology.

## ■ ranked societies

societies in which there is unequal access to prestige and status, e.g. chiefdoms and states.

## ■ reaves

Bronze Age stone boundary walls, for instance on Dartmoor, England, which may designate the territorial extent of individual communities.

## ■ reciprocity

a mode of exchange in which transactions take place between individuals who are symmetrically placed, i.e. they are exchanging as equals, neither being in a dominant position.

## ■ reconnaissance survey

a broad range of techniques involved in the location of archaeological sites, e.g. the recording of surface artefacts and features and the sampling of natural and mineral resources.

■ **records management**

the process involved in determining the status, value and disposition of administrative records throughout their lifetime, active or inactive. Also involves scheduling records for their ultimate disposition.

■ **records**

1. all information fixed in a tangible (textual, electronic, audiovisual or visual) form that was created by an organisation as part of its daily business.

2. two or more data fields that are grouped as a unit in machine-readable records. Federal records are defined as all books, papers, maps, photographs, machine readable materials or other documentary materials, regardless of physical form or characteristics, made or received by an agency of the United States Government under Federal law or in connection with the transaction of public business and preserved or appropriate for preservation by that agency or its legitimate successor as evidence of the organisation, functions, policies, decisions, procedures, operations or other activities of the Government or because of the informational value of data in them.

■ **recurvate**

a shape that from the bottom starts wide, then thins out becomes wide and then again thins out to the distal end. A fish shaped profile. A basal edge that has two smooth indents, with a central excurvate bulge.

■ **red ochre (ochre)**

powdered iron ore placed in a burial area.

■ **redistribution**

a mode of exchange which implies the operation of some central organising authority. Goods are received or appropriated by the central authority and subsequently some of them are

sent by that authority to other locations.
reemay®

# refitting

sometimes referred to as conjoining, this entails attempting to put stone tools and flakes back together again and provides important information on the processes involved in the knapper's craft.

# reformatting

preservation duplication of original archival materials through the use of long-lived copy technology such as silver halide microfilms or large format digital files and computer output microfilms.

# refutationist view

approach which holds that science consists of theories about the empirical world, that its goal is to develop better theories, which is achieved by finding mistakes in existing theories, so that it is crucial that theories be falsifiable (vulnerable to error and open to testing). The approach, developed by Karl Popper, emphasises the importance of testability as a component of scientific theories.

# registrar

an individual responsible for the development and implementation of procedures and policies affecting the acquisition, management and disposition of collections. A registrar also usually maintains all collection documentation, including inventory and loans. Specific duties vary between institutions.

# rehabilitation

to restore to a former state or good condition. In conservation, this applies to the restoration of deteriorated objects. It can also refer to the upgrade of an entire collection.

# rejects

preforms that, because of some unsuitable flaking qualities of the stone or breakage were discarded without being completed.

■ **relative dating**

the determination of chronological sequence without recourse to a fixed time scale, e.g. the arrangement of artefacts in a typological sequence or seriation.

■ **relative humidity (RH)**

the measure of moisture in the air in relation to the saturation point of the air at its current temperature. RH is measured as a percentage of the absolute humidity divided by the saturation humidity.

■ **relativism**

the concept that a cultural system can be viewed only in terms of the principles, background, frame of reference and history that characterise it.

■ **relieving arch**

arch built as part of a solid wall to take the weight of the construction above and to divert it from weak points such as doors and windows lower down revetment. Facing of one material given to a structure of a different material e.g. stonewall given to an earth bank rounded circular panel containing a design, e.g. on mosaics.

■ **religion**

a framework of beliefs relating to supernatural or superhuman beings or forces that transcend the everyday material world.

■ **religious use**

as cited in NAGPRA, '...use in religious rituals or spiritual activities. Religious remains generally are of interest to medicine men and women and other religious practitioners and persons from Indian tribes, Alaskan Native corporations, Native Hawaiians, and other indigenous and immigrant ethnic, social and religious groups that have aboriginal or historic ties to the lands from which the remains are recovered and have traditionally used the remains or class of remains in religious rituals or spiritual activities.'

## ■ remote sensing
general term for reconnaissance and surface survey techniques that leave subsurface archaeological deposits undisturbed.

## ■ renewable resource
natural resource that can be replaced.

## ■ repatriation
to return or restore the control of an object or collection to the country of origin or rightful owner. Used to describe the return of items to lineal descendants or culturally affiliated tribes under NAGPRA.

## ■ replication
the experimental reproduction or duplication of prehistoric artefacts in an attempt to better understand how they were made and used in the past.

## ■ repository
a facility such as a museum, archaeological centre, laboratory or storage facility that is managed by a university, college, museum or other educational or scientific institution, a federal, state or local government agency or Indian tribe that can provide professional, systematic and accountable curatorial services on a long-term basis.

## ■ rescue archaeology
a term applied to the emergency salvage of sites in immediate danger of destruction by major land modification projects such as reservoir construction. See also **salvage archaeology**.

■ **research design**

0systematic planning of research, usually including.
1.the formulation of a strategy to resolve a particular
question.
2.the collection and recording of the evidence.
3.the processing and analysis
of these data and their interpretation.
4. the publication of results.

■ **resharpening flakes**

usually small flakes removed
from the edges of chipped-
stone cutting or scraping
tools to rejuvenate the effec-
tiveness of the edge.

■ **resistivity meter**

natural accretions of manga-
nese and iron oxides, to-
gether with clay minerals and
organic matter, which can
provide valuable environ-
mental evidence. Their study,
when combined with radio-
carbon methods, can pro-
vide a minimum age for
some landforms and even
some types of stone tools

which also accumulate varnish.

■ **resistivity**

a means of detecting buried
features and areas of disturbance by measuring the re-
sistance of an electrical current passed through the
ground.

■ **respect**

set of values which honour
an individual, culture or set
of object.

■ **retouch**

the removal of small secondary flakes along the edge of
a lithic artefact, to improve
or alter the cutting properties of that edge. Retouch
flaking may be bifacial or
unifacial.

■ **retouched flake**

a stone flake which has had
one or more edges modified
by the deliberate removal of
secondary chips.

■ **retouching**

the fine flaking of an edge to
improve and finalise the

form by removal of the small flakes (usually by pressure) to produce sharpness.

# reworking

flaking applied to a broken or dulled tool so as to reclaim it for additional use. Sometimes called lateral rejuvenation, reworking was the characteristic means by which an implement was re-sharpened. Alternate and bifacial bevelling, serration and other diagnostic features of blade renewal are very important to age determination as well as for the purpose of assembling attribute clusters for typological analysis. Typically, reworked blades or points have a different outline than their former pristine outline. Reworking of lithic objects was employed by early man due to the general lack of high quality lithic materials.

# rhizopod

a protozoan of the class Rhizopoda that has pseudopodia.

# rhyolite

a fine-grained, light coloured volcanic rock, chemically identical to obsidian. Colour may range from white, through grey and yellow to reddish-pink. Sometimes used as a raw material for lithic tools.

# rimsherd

a fragment of the rim or top edge, of a ceramic vessel. Important archaeologically since rimsherds frequently show the greatest degree of stylistic variability.

# rind

the deeply patinated or weathered surface of a nodule or other piece of stone, flint, chert or other material.

# risk management

the planning and use of available resources to minimise overall risk to collections. Involves identifying risks, identifying strategies to eliminate or manage risks and setting priorities for risk elimination and management. In repositories, this involves measures for security, fire control, pests and disaster planning.

■ **ritual**

behaviour that has become highly formalised and stereotyped.

■ **road cut**

building of a road in the area.

■ **rock alignment**

any artificial arrangement of rocks or boulders into rows or other patterns.

■ **rock shelter**

a rock overhang used as a shelter by Early Americans.

■ **rock-art**

an inclusive term for petroglyphs and pictographs.

■ **rock-shelter**

a shallow cave or rock overhang, large enough to have allowed human occupancy at some time.

■ **rounded**

a term used to describe a basal edge which has rounded stem outline. Also a term to describe a point which is not sharp or barb types.

■ **rudist**

an extinct bivalve mollusc from the Jurassic and Cretaceous that had two different sised and shaped shells. They usually were attached to the substrate and were either solitary or in reef like masses.

■ **rules**

a set of defined actions permitted in a certain situation or location.

■ **sacellum**

shrine in a fort's headquarters building.

■ **sacred objects**

specific ceremonial objects which are needed by traditional religious leaders for the practice of traditional religions by their present-day adherents. An important component of NAGPRA for American Indians, Native Hawaiians and Native Alaskans.

■ **sacred**

the sphere of extraordinary phenomena associated with awesome supernatural forces.

■ **safety**

set of procedures which keep people or objects in good condition.

■ **salvage archaeology (also 'rescue archaeology' or 'crisis archaeology')**

archaeological research carried out to preserve or rescue sites, materials and data, from areas threatened by man-made or natural disturbance. The most common type of archaeological fieldwork conducted in North America at the present time.

■ **samian**

high-quality, red-coated pottery, imported from the European continent, mainly from France.

■ **sampling bias**

the tendency of a sample to exclude some members of the sampling universe and over-represent others.

■ **sampling error**

in population genetics, the transmission of a non-representative sample of the gene pool over space or time due to chance.

■ **sampling unit**

the sub-element of the total population selected for sampling.

■ **sampling universe**

the largest entity to be described, of which the sample is a part.

■ **sampling**

a process of selecting a representative part of a population for the purpose of determining parameters or characteristics of the whole population. The selection process may be based on a mathematical probability theory, a regularised pattern or existing knowledge of data patterning.

■ **santonian**

European stage of the Upper Cretaceous, spanning the time between 88 and 84 million years ago.

■ **sarcophagus**

coffin of stone or lead.

■ **Saxon Shore**

coast of SE England exposed to Saxon pirate raids.

■ **Scanning Electron Microscope (SEM)**

a microscope in which a finely focussed beam of electrons is scanned across a specimen and the electron intensity variations are used to construct an image of the specimen. This type of microscope is ideal for magnifications from 200 to 35,000.

■ **scapula**

the shoulder bone of an animal.

■ **scarp**

an escarpment, cliff or other steep slope, such as the slope between fluvial terraces.

■ **science**

a method of reaming about the world by applying the principles of the scientific method, which includes making empirical observations, proposing hypotheses to explain those observations and testing those hypotheses in valid and reliable ways. Also refers to the organised body of knowledge that results from scientific study.

■ **scientific theory**

a statement that postulates ordered relationships among natural phenomena.

■ **scientism**

the belief that there is one and only one method of science and that it alone confers legitimacy upon the conduct of research.

■ **scope of collections**

a repository planning document that details the extent of its collections, including what it may acquire in the future to fulfil its mission.

# scoping

in archaeology, it involves determining the extent of a site and what work may be performed on that site. In CRM terms, scoping is done under NEPa and involves determining the extent of the environmental/cultural impact of a proposed action and what can be done about that impact.

# scraper

a stone tool designed for use in scraping hides, bones and other similar materials in the preparation of food, clothing and shelter. A small stone blade with uniface flaking.

# scraper

a tool presumably used in scraping, scouring or planing functions. Most frequently refers to flaked stone artefacts with one or more steep unifacially retouched edge(s).

# secondary burial

a human interment which was moved and re-buried aboriginally.

# secondary datum

a local base measuring point at a known distance from the main horizontal or vertical datum points.

# secondary deposit

a body of natural or cultural sediments which have been disturbed and re-transported since their original deposition.

# secondary retouch

finishing or re-sharpening flaking done after the basic shape of a lithic tool has been completed.

# section

1. a vertical cut (or exposure) through a body of sediments or a feature.
2. a one-square mile unit in the legal subdivision system.

# security copy

duplicate copy of original documentation that is on archival paper and is stored in a separate location from the original.

■ **sedentary**

a term applied to human groups leading a settled, non-migratory lifestyle.

■ **sedentism**

the practice of establishing a permanent, year-round settlement.

■ **sediment**

solid unconsolidated rock and mineral fragments that come from the weathering of rocks and are transported by water, air or ice and form layers on the Earth's surface. Sediments can also result from chemical precipitation or secretion by organisms.

■ **sedimentary beds**

beds or layers of sediments, also called strata.

■ **sedimentary rock**

a rock that is the result of consolidation of sediments.

■ **sedimentation**

the accumulation of geological or organic material deposited by air, water or ice.

■ **sedimentology**

a subset of geomorphology concerned with the investigation of the structure and texture of sediments, i.e. the global term for material deposited on the earth's surface.

■ **segmentary societies**

relatively small and autonomous groups, usually of agriculturalists, who regulate their own affairs. In some cases, they may join together with other comparable segmentary societies to form a larger ethnic unit.

■ **seismic reflection profiler**

an acoustic underwater survey device that uses the principle of echo-sounding to locate submerged landforms. In water depths of 100 m, this method can achieve penetration of more than 10 m into the sea-floor.

■ **selective pressure**

pressure placed by a selective agent upon certain individuals within the population that results in the change of allele frequencies in the next generation.

■ **self-organisation**

the product of a theory derived from thermodynamics which demonstrates that order can arise spontaneously when systems are pushed far from an equilibrium state. The emergence of new structure arises at bifurcation points or thresholds of instability.

■ **self-reducing tacheometer**

a major surveying instrument (transit or alidade) which allows the direct read-out of true vertical and horizontal distances within the eye-piece, without the use of trigonometric formulae or tables.

■ **sensory oriented**

oriented to touch, taste, sound, sight, hearing, heart.

■ **seriation**

a relative dating technique based on the chronological ordering of a group of artefacts or assemblages, where the most similar are placed adjacent to each other in the series. Two types of seriation can be recognised, frequency seriation and contextual seriation.

■ **series**

a group of documents arranged or maintained as a unit within a file system because of their shared circumstances of creation, receipt or use. An example of a list of series would be:

1. incoming correspondence.
2. outgoing correspondence.
3. bills and check receipts.
4. photographs.
5. legal documents.

■ **serrated**

notched or toothed. May refer to the edge of a tool.

■ **serrations**

consecutive small teeth or barbs on the edge of a blade, formed by removing pressure flakes. Biface serrations have flakes removed from both sides of the blade edge while uniface serrations have flakes removed from only one face of an edge.

■ **settlement pattern**

the spatial distribution of cultural activities across a landscape at a given moment in time.

■ **seven wonders of the ancient world**

seven structures and statues that were seen as magnificent and impressive to ancient people. The Seven Wonders included the Colossus of Rhodes, the Hanging Gardens of Babylon, the Temple of Zeus at Olympus, the Temple of Artemis, the Mausoleum, the Pharos (Lighthouse) and the Great Pyramid at Giza.

■ **severus, septimus**

ancient Roman ruler who rebuilt the city of Lepcis Magna.

■ **sexual division of labour**

the situation in which males and females in a society perform different tasks. In hunting-gathering societies males usually hunt while females usually gather wild vegetable food.

■ **shape**

the three dimensional image perceived when one considers the entire artefact.

■ **shell midden**

a site formed of mainly concentrated shellfish remains.

■ **sherds**

the individual pieces of broken pottery vessels.

■ **shoulder**

the area of an artefact that divides the blade from the stem or hafting area.

# shovel-screening

a rapid excavation procedure in which the site matrix is shovelled directly through a screen (usually 1/4' mesh).

# side-blade

a flaked stone, bone, shell or metal artefact inserted in the side of a shaft or projectile point to provide an extended cutting edge.

# sidescan sonar

a survey method used in underwater archaeology which provides the broadest view of the sea-floor. An acoustic emitter is towed behind a vessel and sends out sound waves in a fan-shaped beam. These pulses of sonic energy are reflected back to a transducer— return time depending on distance travelled— and recorded on a rotating drum.

# silica gel

a granular substance which has high moisture absorbing and emitting properties. It is often used as a moisture stabiliser in packing, storing and exhibiting items that are sensitive to humidity.

# silurian

a period of the Palaeozoic, spanning the time between 440 and 410 million years ago. It is named after a Celtic tribe called the Silures.

# simple random sampling

a type of probabilistic sampling where the areas to be sampled are chosen using a table of random numbers. Drawbacks include.

1. defining the site's boundaries beforehand.

2. the nature of random number tables results in some areas being allotted clusters of sample squares, while others remain untouched.

# simulation

the formulation and computer implementation of dynamic models i.e. models concerned with change through time. Simulation is a useful heuristic device and can be of considerable help in the development of explanation.

■ **site**

a location where human activities once took place and left some form of material evidence. A location which has yielded artefacts and either is, has or will undergo excavation or is being conserved for the future. Known sites should not be disturbed by amateurs or surface hunted. Sites can be registered and can have a site number or code associated with them.

■ **Site Catchment Analysis (SCA)**

a type of off-site analysis which concentrates on the total area from which a site's contents have been derived. At its simplest, a site's catchment can be thought of as a full inventory of artefactual and non-artefactual remains and their sources.

■ **site exploitation terri-**

**tory (set)**

often confused with site catchment analysis, this is a method of achieving a fairly standardised assessment of the area habitually used by a site's occupants.

■ **site report**

a document detailing the findings at an archaeological site. Site reports are usually required for archaeological projects conducted on federal, state and tribal lands. They can run from simple statements on what was found to detailed data analysis and interpretation.

■ **site survey**

a non-intrusive method of observing a site without excavation. There are many types of surveys, including pedestrian walkovers, controlled collection and a number of remote sensing procedures such as resistivity, magnetic, radar, side-scan sonar and metal detection surveys. These surveys allow archaeologists to 'see' a buried site or feature without disturbing the ground and guide any needed follow-up investigations such as test excavations, block excavations and other kinds of data retrieval.

# site

1. a location where human activities once took place and left some form of material evidence.

2. a distinct spatial clustering of artefacts, features, structures and organic and environmental remains as the residue of human activity.

# skull deformation

the artificial distortion of cranial bones during growth practiced by some aboriginal cultures.

# slag

the material residue of smelting processes from metalworking. Analysis is often necessary to distinguish slags derived from copper smelting from those produced in iron production. Crucible slags (from the casting process) may be distinguished from smelting slags by their high concentration of copper.

# slar (sideways-looking airborne radar)

a remote sensing technique that involves the recording in radar images of the return of pulses of electromagnetic radiation sent out from aircraft.

# sleeper wall

low wall supporting a raised floor, especially in a granary.

# slope distance

in mapping the inclined distance (as opposed to true horizontal or vertical distance) between 2 points.

# smoothing

an edge that has been worn smooth and rounded from use in scraping or drilling.

# snapped base

a term used to describe points that have a part of the

base intentionally removed or fractured off as part of the intentional design by the original knapper.

**■ snares**
loops of material (vine, fibre, leather, etc) used for catching animals.

**■ snares**
loops of material (vine, fibre, leather, etc) used for catching animals.

**■ social anthropology**
see **cultural anthropology.**

**■ social category**
a category composed of all people who share certain culturally identified characteristics.

**■ social class**
a category of people who have generally similar educational histories, job opportunities and social standing and who are conscious of their membership in a social group that is ranked in relation to others and is replicated over generations.

**■ social control**
a framework of rewards and sanctions that channel behaviour.

**■ society**
a group of interacting people who share a geographical region, a sense of common identity and a common culture.

**■ sociobiology**
the study of the biological control of social behaviour.

**■ sociocultural anthropology**
a branch of anthropology that deals with variations in patterns of social interaction and differences in cultural behaviour.

**■ sociolinguistics**
a branch of anthropological linguistics that studies how language and culture are related and how language is used in different social contexts.

■ **soil resistivity**

a method of subsurface detection which measures changes in conductivity by passing electrical current through ground soils. This is generally a consequence of moisture content and in this way, buried features can be detected by differential retention of groundwater.

■ **soil scientist**

one who studies the distribution, fertility and chemical and organic composition of the upper layer of earth.

■ **soil texture**

the relative proportion of clay, silt and sand sised particles in a soil.

■ **soil-sieves**

small, precision metal screens, used for determining the proportions of different sised particles in a soil sediment sample.

■ **soil-sounding radar**

a method of subsurface detection in which short radio pulses are sent through the soil, such that the echoes reflect back significant changes in soil conditions.

■ **solifluction**

the slow downslope movement of surface sediments in a saturated condition. Prevalent in permafrost areas due to the seasonal thawing of the surface of the permafrost zone. Can cause complete mixture of site stratigraphy and archaeological components.

■ **soluble salt**

type of salt (including chlorides, nitrates and sulphates) that is readily soluble in water. Can be absorbed by any porous material buried in soil that contains these salts. When evaporation occurs, salts crystallise on or near an object's surface and can lead to its destruction.

■ **solvent**

a substance capable of dissolving another substance.

Solvents are often liquids and tend to be volatile. Different solvents are needed for dissolving different substances, depending on chemical composition. A common solvent is acetone.

■ **spalling**
delaminating or breaking off into chips and pieces. Spalling is often caused in archaeological materials by subflorescence.

■ **spalls**
the unused flakes left from flint knapping.

■ **spear point**
a large projectile that was probably designed to be hafted onto a long, hand held shaft.

■ **specialisation**
the limited range of activities in which a single individual is likely to be engaged.

■ **spheres of exchange**
the modes of exchange—reciprocity, redistribution and market exchange—that apply to particular goods or in particular situations.

■ **spokeshave**
an artefact with a notch or concave edge, presumed to have been used in shaping wooden or bone shafts.

■ **springer**
the voussoir which rests on the cap above a jamb and marks the beginning of an arch stoke-hole. Furnace-area for a hypocaust.

■ **stadia rod (also 'surveyor's staff')**
a long brightly painted rod, accurately calibrated in metric units or feet and inches, used for obtaining elevations and stadia measurements of distance in mapping with a major surveying instrument.

■ **stage**

a complex developmental unit encompassing a broad span of time, widespread of cultural unity and cultural sequences.

■ **standing wave technique**

an acoustic method, similar to bosing, used in subsurface detection.

■ **state archaeologist**

an appointed official who is responsible for overseeing all potential impacts to archaeological resources and for reviewing and administering all archaeological work in order to insure compliance with state and federal regulations.

■ **State Historic Preservation Office (SHPO)**

established by the National Historic Preservation Act of 1966 as an agency within each state government, charged with enforcing the provisions of the Act. SHPO receive, federal funds from the National Park Service and allocate matching funds and grants to local agencies and private citizens for the protection of sites eligible for listing in the National Register of Historic Places.

■ **State Historic Preservation Officer (SHPO)**

the state official, designated by the governor, to carry out the functions ascribed to the SHPO under the National Historic Preservation Act. SHPOs receive and administer matching grants from NPS to support their work and pass through to others. They identify historic properties and nominate them to the National Register. They maintain inventories, do plans and consult with others about historic preservation.

■ **state**

a term used to describe a social formation defined by distinct territorial boundary and characterised by strong central government in which the operation of political power is sanctioned by legitimate force. In cultural evolutionist models, it ranks second only to the empire as the most complex societal development stage.

# statistical analysis

the application of probability theory to quantified descriptive data.

# status

a position in a pattern of reciprocal behaviour.

# steatite

1. a greyish-green or brownish type of soapstone quarried for the purpose of manufacturing bowls, pipes and ornaments. The soapstone is carveable and shapeable which lends itself to use especially before the invention of pottery.

2. soapstone or talc. A soft grey to green stone used as a carving medium.

# stela (pl. stelae)

a free-standing carved stone monument.

# stem

the extension of the base of a projectile point or knife which was designed for hafting or gripping. Stems can occur in various shapes.

# stemmed point

a projectile or blade that has a stem which was designed for hafting or holding.

# step-trenching

an excavation method employed on very deep sites, such as Near Eastern tell sites, in which the excavation proceeds downwards in a series of gradually narrowing steps.

# stereoscope

a simple optical device to allow the perception of a stereoscopic or 3-dimensional image from pairs of aerial photographs.

# sticky traps

a passive insect or rodent trap that uses an adhesive to trap the pest.

# stone boiling

a type of cooking that is done by heating stones in an open fire and then placing them in the liquid or substance to be cooked. This is often done in baskets or containers that cannot be placed directly in or over a fire.

# storage-pit (also called cache-pits)

circular excavations, usually less than 3 m in diameter, assumed to have aboriginally functioned as storage 'cellars'.

# story board

written and visual representation outlining a concept.

# strata

1. layers of soil or earth.
2. depositional units or layers of sediment distinguished by composition or appearance. (singular: 'stratum').
3. individually sampled subareas in a 'stratified-random' probabilistic sampling scheme.

# stratification

the laying down or depositing of strata or layers (also called deposits) one above the other. A succession of layers should provide a relative chronological sequence, with the earliest at the bottom and the latest at the top.

# ■ stratified random sampling

a form of probabilistic sampling in which the region or site is divided into natural zones or strata such as cultivated land and forest. Units are then chosen by a random number procedure, so as to give each zone a number of squares proportional to its area, thus overcoming the inherent bias in simple random sampling.

# ■ stratified sample

a sample obtained by the process of dividing a population into categories representing distinctive characteristics and then selecting a random sample from each category.

# ■ stratified society

a society in which extensive subpopulations are accorded differential treatment.

# ■ stratified systematic sampling

a form of probabilistic sampling which combines the elements of:

1. simple random sampling.
2. stratified random sampling.
3. systematic sampling, in an effort to reduce sampling bias.

# ■ stratigraphy

1. the study of layers sequentially deposited over time, the arrangement of strata with respect to the position in which they were laid down by human occupation or from natural causes. This is very helpful for land archaeology. Under water, it can also be useful, but it is more complicated and often confusing because of current and sea movement.

2. the study and validation of stratification. The analysis in the vertical time dimension, of a series of layers in the horizontal space dimension. It is often used as a relative dating

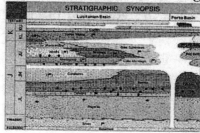

technique to assess the temporal sequence of artefact deposition.

■ **street-grid**

regular pattern of streets crossing at right-angles.

■ **striking platform**

a prepared basal edge of a projectile point. This edge is bevelled to a degree of pitch that will allow a drift to be set at the proper angle to strike off a channel flake.

■ **structural functionalism**

the theory that the central function of the various aspects of a society is to maintain the social structure—the society's pattern of social relations and institutions.

■ **structuralist approaches**

interpretations which stress that human actions are guided by beliefs and symbolic concepts and that underlying these are structures of thought which find expression in various forms. The proper object of study is therefore to uncover the structures of thought and to study their influence in shaping the ideas in the minds of the human actors who created the archaeological record.

■ **study or type collection**

a collection of archaeological items that represents a certain class of objects, usually demonstrating the typical or the range of variation. It may be compiled for the purpose of comparison in order to advance scholarly research.

■ **style**

according to the art historian, Ernst Gombrich, style is 'any distinctive and therefore recognisable way in which an act is performed and made'. Archaeologists and anthropologists have defined 'stylistic areas' as areal units representing shared ways of producing and decorating artefacts.

# ■ sub-bottom profiler
see **underwater reconnaissance**.

# ■ sub-disciplines
biological (physical) anthropology, cultural (social) anthropology, archaeology and anthropological linguistics.

# ■ subsistence economy
the means by which a group obtains the food and shelter necessary to support life.

# ■ subsistence pattern
the basic means by which a human group extracted and utilised energy from its environment.

# ■ subsurface detection
a collective name for a variety of remote sensing techniques operating at ground level and including hosing (or bowsing), augering, magnetometer and radar techniques.

# ■ subtropical
bordering on the tropics or nearly tropical.

# ■ sudatorium
hot room (dry heat) in a bath-suite.

# ■ superposition
the principle that under stable conditions, strata on the bottom of a deposit were laid down first and hence are older than layers on top.

# ■ surface collection
archaeological materials obtained from the ground surface.

# ■ surface finish
in the study of ceramic artefacts, the mainly decorative outer elements of a vessel.

# ■ surface scatter
archaeological materials found distributed over the ground surface.

# ■ surface survey
two basic kinds can be identified: unsystematic and systematic. The former involves

field-walking, i.e. scanning the ground along one's path and recording the location of artefacts and surface features. Systematic survey by comparison is less subjective and involves a grid system, such that the survey area is divided into sectors and these are walked systematically, thus making the recording of finds mote accurate.

# ■ survey area

the region within which archaeological sites are to be located.

# ■ survey

the process of locating archaeological sites and features over a specific area. It is the first step (Phase I) in archaeological reconnaissance that usually involves mapping the site, as well as any artefacts and features. Some artefacts may be collected depending on the field collecting strategy of the project.

# ■ surveying

(1) in archaeology, the process of locating archaeological sites. (2) more generally, the process of mapping and measuring points on the ground surface e.g. 'legal' or topographic surveying'.

# ■ symbol

something that can represent something distant from it in time and space.

# ■ symmetry analysis

a mathematical approach to the analysis of decorative style which claims that patterns can be divided into two distinct groups or symmetry classes: 17 classes for those patterns that repeat motifs horizontally and 46 classes for those that repeat them horizontally and vertically. Such studies have suggested that the choice of motif arrangement within a particular culture is far from random.

■ **synchronic studies**
rely on research that does not make use of or control for the effects of the passage of time.

■ **synchronic**
referring to phenomena considered at a single point in time, i.e. an approach which is not primarily concerned with change.

■ **synostosis**
the joining of separate pieces of bone in human skeletons. The precise timing of such processes is an important indicator of age.

■ **synthetic theory of evolution**
the theory of evolution that fuses Darwin's concept of natural selection with information from the fields of genetics, mathematics, embryology, palaeontology, animal behaviour and other disciplines.

■ **system**
a series of interrelated parts wherein a change in one part brings about changes in all parts.

■ **systematic sampling**
a form of probabilistic sampling employing a grid of equally spaced locations; e.g. selecting every other square. This method of regular spacing runs the risk of missing (or hitting) every single example if the distribution itself is regularly spaced.

■ **systematic survey**
see **surface survey**.

■ **systems thinking**
a method of formal analysis in which the object of study is viewed as comprising distinct analytical sub-units. Thus, in archaeology, it comprises a form of explanation in which a society or culture is seen through the interaction and interdependence of its component parts. These

are referred to as system parameters and may include such things as population size, settlement pattern, crop production, technology, etc.

■ **tang**
a projection that extends from the base or stem of a point, also known as ears.

■ **taphonomy**
the study of processes which have affected organic materials such as bone after death. It also involves the microscopic analysis of toothmarks or cut marks to assess the effects of butchery or scavenging activities.

■ **taxonomy**
the science dealing with the identification, naming and classification of plants and animals.

■ **tectonic movements**
displacements in the plates that make up the earth's crust, often responsible for the occurrence of raised beaches.

■ **tectonic plate**
a segment of the lithosphere.

■ **teflon monofilament**
type of archival quality string that is often used to attach tags to objects because of its non-abrasive, non-damaging qualities.

■ **tell**
a Near Eastern term that refers to a mound site formed through successive human occupation over a very long timespan.

■ **temper**
the use of an additive, i.e. ground shell, to both strengthen and reduce shrinking of ceramics during firing.

■ **tempering agent**
sand, stone, shell, clay or plant fibres added to local clays to prevent pottery from shrinkage and cracking during firing or drying.

■ **tempering agent**
materials added to clay in the manufacture of ceramic artefacts, to prevent cracking

during firing. Could include vegetal fibres, feathers, rock fragments, sand or ground-up pot-sherds.

■ **tent-ring**
a circle of rocks used to hold down the edges of an aboriginal tent, e.g. 'tipi-rings'.

■ **tephra**
volcanic ash. In the Mediterranean, for example, deep-sea coring produced evidence for the ash fall from the eruption of theta and its stratigraphic position provided important information in the construction of a relative chronology.

■ **tepidarium**
warm room with moist heat in a bath-suite.

■ **terrace**
a fluvial terrace is a remnant of an earlier flood-plain isolated by down-cutting of the river, resulting in a step-like series of 'flats' and scarps. Beach terraces are old, ocean or lake beaches, isolated by lowered water levels.

■ **terrestrial**
referring to land habitats in distinction from water (aquatic) habitats.

■ **territory**
the familiar surroundings or home range which is claimed by a group of people.

■ **tertiary**
the first period of the Cenozoic era (after the Mesozoic era and before the Quaternary period), spanning the time between 65 and 1.8 million years ago.

■ **tesseera**
a small tablet (as of wood, bone or ivory) used by the ancient Romans as a ticket, tally, voucher or means of identifi-

cation, or a small piece (as of marble, glass or tile) used in mosaic work.

## ■ tessellated

composed of tesserae, usually of a floor without decoration tesserae small cubes of coloured stone, glass or tile, of which a mosaic or tessellated floor is composed.

## ■ test excavation

subsurface excavations in areas which are either defined as sites based on surface artefacts or thought to contain buried deposits based on the landform.

## ■ test pit (also 'test excavation')

a small exploratory 'dig' designed to determine a site's depth and contents, prior to major excavation.

## ■ Texas Archaeological Research Laboratory

a branch of the university of Texas at Austin that has been appointed as the official state registry for archaeological sites and the repository for archaeological collections.

## ■ theodolite (also 'optical transit')

a transit with accurate optical readout of vertical and horizontal angles.

## ■ theory

a step in the scientific method in which a statement is generated on the basis of highly confirmed hypothesis and is used to generalise about conditions not yet tested.

## ■ thermal prospection

a remote sensing method used in aerial reconnaissance. It is based on weak variations in temperature, which can be found above buried structures whose thermal properties are different from those of their surroundings.

## ■ thermography

a non-photographic technique which uses thermal or heat sensors in aircraft to record the temperature of the soil surface. Variations in soil temperature can be the result of the presence of buried structures.

# thermoluminescence dating (tl)

a chronometric dating method based on the fact that some materials, when heated, give off a flash of light. The intensity of the light is proportional to the amount of radiation the sample has been exposed to and the length of time since the sample was heated. It has much in common with electron spin resonance (ESR).

# thermoplastic acrylic

a polymer that is applied as a liquid and then hardens or sets. They are resoluble in an appropriate solvent and soften upon heating.

# thermosetting resin

resins that change (irreversibly) under heat, from a fusible, soluble material, into one that is infusible and insoluble, through the formation of a covalently cross-linked, thermally stable network.

# thickness

a measurement take at the thickest point.

# Thiessen polygons

a formal method of describing settlement patterns based on territorial divisions centred on a single site. The polygons are created by drawing straight lines between pairs of neighbouring sites, then at the mid-point along each of these lines, a second series of lines are drawn at right angles to the first. Linking the second series of lines creates the Thiessen polygons.

# thinning

decreasing the thickness of an artefact or a portion of an artefact by extensive flaking. Basal thinning refers to the removal of thickness from the hafting area by means of flake removal.

# ■ thin-section analysis

a technique whereby microscopic thin sections are cut from a stone object or potsherd and examined with a petrological microscope to determine the source of the material.

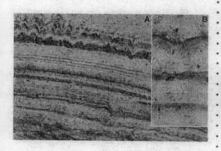

# ■ three age system

a classification system devised by C.J. Thomsen for the sequence of technological periods (stone, bronze and iron) in Old World prehistory. It established the principle that by classifying artefacts, one could produce a chronological ordering.

# ■ till

sediments laid down directly by glacial ice. Commonly consists of unsorted angular rock fragments mixed with clay.

# ■ timber frame

an early English building technique using sawn or hewn lumber (cut using hand tools) and joined with mortises and tenons (holes and pegs) instead of nails.

# ■ tipi

a relatively large conical skin and pole tent used in the Plains area.

# ■ titulum

short detached stretch of rampart (and ditch) protecting the gateway of a marching camp.

## ■ tomb

a structure, either above or underground, used to house a dead body.

## ■ tool kit

the set of all weapons and tools that was created and used by a person or group of people.

## ■ topographic map

a map which accurately depicts the physical features and relief of an area.

## ■ topography

study of land features at a site. This can be useful in determining the potential of an archaeological site for excavation.

## ■ totem

a plant or animal associated with a clan as a means of group identification. It may have other significance for the group as well.

## ■ township

a square area, containing 36 sections. A major unit of the legal subdivision system.

## ■ trace element analysis

the use of chemical techniques, such as neutron activation analysis or X-ray fluorescence spectrometry, for determining the incidence of trace elements in rocks. These methods are widely used in the identification of raw material sources for the production of stone tools.

## ■ tradition

a continuum of gradational culture change through time representing the unbroken development of a single culture.

## ■ trait

1. any artefact or recognisable characteristic that reflects human activity or behaviour.
2. any discrete cultural element or one aspect of the phenotype.

## ■ trajectory

in systems thinking, this refers to the series of successive states through which the system proceeds over time. It may be said to represent the long-term behaviour of the system.

## ■ transcript

a record of a conversation. Transcripts may be obtained from interviews, trials or someone's recollections.

## ■ transect

a linear sampling area.

## ■ transit

a sophisticated optical surveying instrument similar to an alidade, except that it is mounted directly on a tripod, rather than resting on a plane.

## ■ transitional

a term used to describe an artefact that was utilised and manufactured across two or more cultural periods.

## ■ transitional paleo

a cultural period of north American aborigine Indians, dating from 12,000 to 9,000 b.p., which occurred between the paleo and archaic periods.

## ■ transverse line

an imaginary line extending across the centre of a projectile, halfway between the distal tip and the basal edge.

## ■ tree-ring dating

a chronometric dating method in which the age of a wood sample is determined by counting the number of annual growth rings.

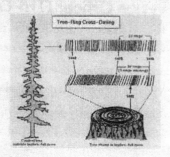

# ■ trend surface analysis

the aim of trend surface analysis is to highlight the main features of a geographic distribution by smoothing over some of the local irregularities. In this way, important trends can be isolated from the background 'noise' more clearly.

# ■ triangular

a projectile, knife, preform or blade which has three sides or roughly has the shape of a triangle.

# ■ triassic

the earliest period of the Mesozoic era, spanning the time between 248 and 213 million years ago. The name Triassic refers to the threefold division of rocks of this age in Germany.

# ■ Tribal Historic Preservation Officer (THPO)

the official of a federally recognised Indian tribe that oversees the tribe's historic preservation program, particularly where the tribe has been approved by NPS to carry out all or some of the functions of the SHPO within the external boundaries of its reservation.

# ■ tribe

a descent and kinship-based group in which subgroups are clearly linked to one another, with the potential of uniting a large number of local groups for common defence or warfare. Unlike bands, tribes are usually settled farmers, though they also include nomadic pastoral groups whose economy is based on exploitation of livestock. Individual communities tend to be integrated into the larger society through kinship ties.

# ■ tribunal

platform for commanding officer in principia or on a parade-ground.

■ **triclinium**
dining-room.

■ **tripolitic weathering**
a severe form of patination where flint or chert seem to be transformed over a long period of time into a chalky, porous, crumbly or granular limestone. It is believed that weathering effects, especially acidic water, can cause this type of transformation.

■ **tropical**
referring to climatic conditions like those found in the region on the earth today, between the tropic of Cancer and the tropic of Capricorn. It includes high temperature and humidity and abundant rainfall.

■ **tuff**
geological formation composed of compressed volcanic ash.

■ **tundra**
a type of landscape where the ground is frozen solid throughout most of the year but thaws slightly during the summer.

■ **turonian**
European stage of the Upper Cretaceous, spanning the time between 91 and 90 million years ago.

■ **tuyere**
a ceramic blowtube used in the process of smelting.

■ **type**
1. a form of projectile or knife for which a description, name and age have been attributed to.
2. a distinctive formal artefact class defined by the consistent clustering of attributes and restricted in space and time, e.g. the 'Folsom Point' is a projectile point 'type'.

## type collection
see **study collection**.

## typology
the study of and the chronological arrangement of projectile points and other lithic artefacts into separated types on the basis of shared attributes.

## ultraviolet (uv) rays
light rays, not visible to the human eye, that can cause permanent damage through fast colour degradation, structural weakening and embrittlement of objects. UV rays are found in natural sunlight and in some artificial light sources (such as fluorescent lamps).

## ulu
an Eskimo word for a relatively large, semi-lunate, side-mounted 'woman's knife'.

## unbevelled
an edge which was not steeply flaked into a bevel.

## unconformity
the surface of a stratum that represents a break in the stratigraphic sequence.

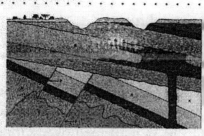

## underwater archaeology
strictly, this means archaeology under water, which is the main discipline of maritime archaeology. However, the term underwater archaeology is often used in a wider sense, also covering maritime and nautical archaeology, not necessarily under water.

## underwater reconnaissance
geophysical methods of underwater survey include.

1. a proton magnetometer towed behind a survey vessel, so as to detect iron and steel objects which distort the earth's magnetic field.
2. sidescan sonar that transmits sound waves in a fan-shaped beam to produce a

graphic image of surface features on the sea-bed.

3. a sub-bottom profiler that emits sound pulses which bounce back from features and objects buried beneath the sea floor.

## ▪ unflaked

a face which was unaltered by applying flaking.

## ▪ unfluted

a term referring to projectile or tool which did not have a channel flake removed to from a flute.

## ▪ uniface

a term used to describe a point or tool that is worked or finished or knapped on only one side or face. When used to describe a projectile cross-section, it means a projectile that has one flat side

and one excurvate or rounded side similar to one half of an ellipse.

## ▪ uniface

a stone artefact flaked only on one surface.

## ▪ unifacial flaking

the removal of secondary flakes from only one surface of a stone nucleus.

## ▪ uniformitarianism

the principle which states that physical forces working to-day to alter the earth were also in force and working in the same way in former times.

## ▪ uranium series dating

a dating method based on the radioactive decay of isotopes of uranium. It has proved particularly useful for the period before 50,000 years ago, which lies outside the time range of radiocarbon dating.

## ▪ use-wear

polish, striations, breakage or minor flaking which develop on a tool's edge during use. Microscopic examination and study of the wear may indicate the past function of tools.

### ■ utilised flake

a stone flake used for a tool without deliberate retouch, but exhibiting use-wear.

### ■ utilised material

pieces of stone that have been used without modification.

### ■ valanginian

European stage of the Lower Cretaceous, spanning the time between 131 and 122 million years ago.

### ■ values

a set of beliefs a person holds to be important to him or her.

### ■ variable

any property that may be displayed in different forms.

### ■ variant

a term used in projectile typology to describe a variation of a type.

### ■ varves

fine layers of alluvium sediment deposited in glacial lakes. Their annual deposition makes them a useful source of dating.

### ■ vein quartz

a relatively pure type of quartz which is found in veins in areas of igneous rocks.

### ■ vendian

the latest period of the Proterozoic era, spanning the time between 650 and 544 million years ago. Sometimes referred to as the Ediacaran period, the Vendian is distinguished by fossils, representing a characteristic collection of complex soft-bodied organisms found at several localities around the world.

# ventral

the front or bottom side of an animal or artefact.

# venus figurines

small Upper Palaeolithic statues, characterised by exaggerated breasts and buttocks and very stylised heads, hands and feet.

# vertical angle

in mapping, the angle of sight measured on the vertical plane.

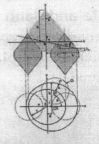

# vertical circle

with major surveying instruments, the graduated vertical table around which the sighting telescope rotates. Used to measure the vertical angle.

# vertical datum

a base measurement point from which all elevations are determined.

# vertical distance

the measurement of distance (or elevations) on a true vertical plane.

# vertical provenience

the vertical position of objects within a site determined in relation to a vertical datum or datum plane, as well as to the local ground surface.

# vexillalion fortress

campaign base for legionaries and auxiliaries.

# vexillatio

detachment of a legion (normally 1,000 men).

# via decumana

road in a fort, running from the back of principia to the back gate.

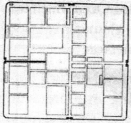

■ **via principalis**

road in a fort linking the gates in the long sides and passing in front of the principia.

■ **vicus**

small civilian settlement, especially one outside a fort.

■ **vizier**

ancient Egyptian prime minister.

■ **volcanic ash**

layers of airborne pumice resulting from violent volcanic eruptions. Provide valuable dating markers when found in sites.

■ **voussoir**

wedge-shaped stone forming one of the units of an arch.

■ **wall-walk**

level platform for the sentry on top of a fortification.

■ **warping**

bending or twisting of a material. Warping is a destructive process that is common to some archaeological materials when they undergo wide fluctuations of relative humidity and temperature.

■ **wattle-and-daub**

wall-construction consisting of wickerwork plastered with mud.

■ **weathering zone**

in pedology, the depth to which soil processes are operational.

■ **weathering**

the natural chemical or physical alteration of an object or deposit through time.

■ **weeping**

slimy, wet surface of a material (usually glass) caused by water migrating and being held on the surface of an object by hygroscopic salts.

■ **weir**

an aboriginal fish-trap based on a fence or barrier of stakes or rocks built across a stream.

■ **welded tuff**

a rock formed of consolidated pumice or volcanic ash. Occasionally used as a raw material for lithic artefacts.

■ **wheeler box-grid**

an excavation technique developed by Mortimer Wheeler from the work of Pitt-Rivers, involving the retaining of intact baulks of earth between excavation grid squares, so that different layers can be correlated across the site in the vertical profiles.

■ **wildlife**

animals living in the wild.

■ **wing**

same as barb.

■ **wisconsin(an) glaciation**

the latest major episode of glacial advance in the Pleistocene of North America, from about 70,000 to 10,000 b.p.

# ■ woodland

a cultural period of the eastern north American aborigine Indians, dating from 3,000 - 1,300 b.p. Usually, the presence of pottery differentiates the woodland culture from the archaic culture which preceded it.

# ■ woodland culture

culture of prehistoric Native Americans in northeast Iowa.

# ■ worked

a term used in projectile point descriptions which describes an area of an artefact that has been shaped or altered by man, such as the removal of flakes along a blade edge.

# ■ working period farm

a term usually associated with a working museum exhibit in which a full scale farm has been restored or reconstructed to depict the former lifeways, tools and technologies of particular periods.

# ■ world system

a term coined by the historian Wallerstein to designate an economic unit, articulated by trade networks extending far beyond the boundaries of individual political units, i.e. nation states and linking them together in a larger functioning unit.

# ■ x-radiography

uses X-rays and film to form an image of objects (and their interior composition) that are otherwise opaque in ultraviolet and visible light. Used on archaeological objects as a non-destructive method for looking at the interior structure of an item, such as corroded metals, statues and complex ceramics.

# ■ x-ray diffraction analysis

a technique used in identifying minerals present in artefact raw materials. It can also be used in geo-morphological contexts to identify particular clay minerals in sediments and thus the specific source from which the sediment was derived.

# ■ X-ray Fluorescence Spectrometry (XRF)

a method used in the analysis of artefact composition, in which the sample is irradiated with a beam of X-rays which excite electrons associated with atoms on the surface.

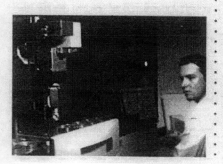

# ■ xtent modelling

a method of generating settlement hierarchy, that overcomes the limitations of both central place theory and Thiessen polygons. It assigns territories to centres based on their scale, assuming that the size of each centre is directly proportional to its area of influence. Hypothetical political maps may thus be constructed from survey data.

# ■ zooarchaeology

the study of faunal remains found in archaeological sites and their cultural significance.

# ■ zoology

a branch of biology that is concerned with the scientific study of animals, including their biology, distribution and identification.

# ■ zoomorphic

'animal-like', refers to artwork or decorated objects with an animal motif or appearance.

# NOTES